THE PRACTICAL GUIDE TO
Children's
Handwriting

Rosemary Sassoon

Hodder & Stoughton

A MEMBER OF THE HODDER HEADLINE GROUP

FRONTISPIECE
The progression of one child's handwriting from 5 to 15
years old, taken from her annual holiday diary. It
demonstrates that, whatever model is imposed,
personal style will usually win in the end.

British Library Cataloguing in Publication Data

ISBN 0 340 630965
First published in 1983 by Thames and Hudson and reprinted in 1989.
Revised edition published by Hodder and Stoughton Educational in 1995.

Impression number 10 9 8 7 6 5 4 3 2 1
Year   1999 1998 1997 1996 1995

Phototypeset by Southern Positives and Negatives (SPAN), Lingfield, Surrey.
Printed in Great Britain for Hodder & Stoughton Educational, a division of
Hodder Headline Plc, 338 Euston Road, London NW1 3BH
by Bath Colour Books, East Kilbride, Scotland.

Contents

PART THREE: CHRONOLOGICAL

Introduction

Handwriting is a skill that modern technology will not replace for some time to come. In early years the child needs writing for recording and communication. Later on, and more important still, writing is the medium through which children and then adults express most of their thinking and ultimately much of their creativity.

A good hand is a pleasure and an asset for life. Learning to write properly need not be a problem, given a good method from the start plus motivation and imaginative teaching. Then it becomes a rewarding, satisfying exercise, and its visible progress a help in all school work. Good handwriting builds confidence in the less able as well as assisting the fast intelligent thinkers to fulfil their promise.

In the rush to literacy and early creative writing during the first years of school, not nearly enough attention is paid to the proper teaching of handwriting as a skill. The current lack of method impairs the children's eventual ability by allowing them to develop bad habits of both writing grip and letter formation. Once implanted, these are hard to break. Unless the correct point of entry and direction of stroke for each letter is taught, understood and used from the start, it is progressively difficult to alter the wrong writing movement that is practised and becomes habitual; and the development of simple ligatures and eventually a legible cursive hand becomes less attainable.

This should be the concern of every parent and teacher. To deprive a child of such an essential skill on the often-heard excuse that the training is repressive, is muddled thinking.

I would like this book to be a reference for teachers and all who work with children. It suggests a commonsense, progressive teaching method based on stroke analysis, with pattern, letter pattern and word sequences, and parallel remedial exercises. There are practical suggestions for many of the common faults that are encountered at different ages, and these faults are put into perspective while considering children's ultimate and individual needs. Skill training is balanced with the equally important need for freedom of style.

1. The aims and priorities of teaching handwriting

The children's eventual handwriting needs must be taken into consideration from the start. The priorities are legibility, speed and the freedom of a personal hand.

Legibility must come first. Handwriting is a means of communication. It must be easy to read, with the letters properly formed, ligatures recognizable and the writing even and well spaced. After that, it must be accepted that there will be two or three different levels of writing required in life as well as at school: a very fast, perhaps scribbled hand for lists and notes, a clear quick hand for essays and examinations, and a more formal hand for special occasions and purposes – such as letters of application, invitations, display work, etc. For better or worse, our personalities are reflected in our handwriting, and certainly in schools writing is taken as an outward indication of progress and as a measure of maturity.

Speed must be the second priority. Our educational systems are geared to note-taking and examinations. Children should be able to write fast enough to do justice to themselves and their knowledge. The fastest print can never really compete with cursive (or joined-up). Although many people do manage quite adequately throughout life with quick print, the objective for children should be cursive. It is therefore necessary to insist on the correct movement from the earliest days in order to ensure smooth progress to a flowing hand. Children mature at different ages, so training must be progressive, and like all lessons it can be either repressive or satisfying, according to the method and the teacher.

Promoting a personal hand My third priority may be considered more controversial. I believe that no child should be forced to follow a model too closely, however good it may be, nor kept too long to the approved school style.

The problem is to balance the need for a model for movement and ligature training, and to get the best out of each of the very different models in use today, with the need to let every child develop his own hand as soon as he is able. This means that teachers must be aware of the individual's progress and have an understanding of letter forms. No imposed hand can be as fast or consistent as a natural hand. Furthermore, imposition of a school model against a pupil's natural inclination can lead to a real repression of creativity and quite unnecessary tensions. To break away from a model is to make progress, and a sign of maturity, not rebellion.

I have omitted beauty as a priority. As many scribes have written: beauty in writing should not be consciously sought after – it should emerge as a result of doing things correctly.

When children have attained a good flowing hand, and are in secondary school, then is the time to expose them to the classic hands of the past to attract those who like them. However, children are just as likely to be influenced by the writing style of a favourite teacher or friend, or to prefer a plain practical hand. Beauty is in the eye of the beholder and this saying is never more true than when discussing handwriting.

I cannot think this ~ providing for
By storm or fish or scale of the .
Walking the sea so h s something gr.

Two contrasting 16-year-olds' writing, both doing their job well.

With these priorities established, it is easy to see where the greatest responsibility lies. The teaching of handwriting is the job of the primary schools. The hand should be flowing and natural by the age of 11 to enable a child to deal with the pressures of secondary school work. Within the primary school the key person must surely be the reception teacher, who starts the child on the way.

Many children start school with faults in letter construction and pencil grip firmly implanted although they may write little more than the letters in their own names. With these much repeated, seldom corrected letters, the writing habits of a lifetime may be formed. The moment a child reaches a formal teaching situation, whether 5 or 6 years old, is crucial. The infant teacher requires not only a good method of teaching from the start, but a knowledge of how to develop individual remedial exercises. It is no good expecting proud parents to correct their pre-school children's first efforts, and anyhow too much correction might well stifle any early creative attempts. I feel, however, that the rules of pre-writing skill training should be available to play-group leaders: the importance of light, posture, pencil grip and paper position for both left- and right-handers, and that pattern exercises should be used to teach the correct formation of letters. With under-5s I would confine corrections to those letters in the children's names.

In today's crowded classrooms there must be sympathy for the overworked teacher, with pressure for visible progress of all sorts from parents as well as from within the school system. However, once the growing child's needs are realized, the priorities must be established within the curriculum. Skill-writing lessons are needed from the start, separate from and complementing creative writing sessions. Standards of handwriting in these two classes will always differ, though with good teaching the gap should eventually narrow.

Few, if any, subjects that are badly taught have such an adverse effect on a child as handwriting. Skill training is specialized, and the teaching of it needs understanding.

I am not suggesting that we return to the dictatorial methods of Victorian days – totally unacceptable today, but nonetheless excellent for training in the correct movement for what was an exceptionally difficult style. Then everyone was doing the same thing at the same time and constant repetition quickly showed up faults to be corrected. As in any other skill, if there is not total obedience to master and model, some way must be found in today's classrooms for a modicum of one-to-one teaching to detect and correct individual incipient faults.

Good teachers and disciplinarians, having accepted this necessity, find little difficulty in organizing their classes into groups to ensure this occasional individual instruction. What really worries me, after several years of specific research into handwriting problems in schools, is the indifference of so many teachers to these very problems. Young teachers, who themselves have survived the system, see no importance in skill training and the damage they are doing to young children is not evident until several years later. Those who train teachers are just as guilty. After thirty years of official disregard, they are giving no priority to the teaching of handwriting. Unless parents, along with informed and concerned teachers, make a concerted stand, there will be another generation unable to write properly, and longer still before the re-instatement of any sort of skill training.

Writing is both a motor and a craft skill whose training has much in common with that of music. Perhaps it is hard for those less strong on the aesthetic side of their natures to see handwriting training as important, and doubly difficult to see the picture as a whole, together with the less obvious side of children's deprivation. Those priorities that *are* stressed are too often neatness and style. It is difficult to explain, the way things are today, that a classroom wall covered with tidy, precise examples of 6- or 7-year-old children's print is counter-productive, and that, on the whole, movement in writing is preferable to neatness. After neatness too much emphasis is put on style, which often only disguises the teacher's lack of any method. The teacher distorts, or lets the child distort, the model to such an extent that its original purpose is often lost. Worse still, the school model can be used as a repressive disciplinary weapon. In some schools a different model can be seen in use in parallel classes as well as consecutive years, and little thought is given to the children forced to move from school to school in our mobile society.

The whole basis of teaching writing from the beginning with static print, which requires retraining to a different writing movement later on, is against children's interest. Flowing, separate letters are quite within the capabilities of 5-year-olds, and lead naturally into cursive as the child matures.

I reaffirm my sympathies with the primary school teacher who has to be an expert in so many fields, but a clear method as I suggest here, which works irrespective of model, can make the teaching of handwriting a rewarding and easier task for all concerned.

At present the remedial services are not considered until the child is 8 years old and the damage has gone too far. Too many children slip through the net entirely, unless they have multiple learning problems, and fall to the level of remedial classes in secondary schools through no fault of their own. In secondary schools there is seldom either time or facilities for dealing with handwriting and intelligent children can fall further and further behind in their work. Of course there will always be a pool of children with multiple problems, but these certainly should be helped by simple, corrective exercises to sort out some of their handwriting problems, removing perhaps the most easily curable of the obstacles to their progress. A good handwriting is often an attainable goal for the less able, and an invaluable tool in the search for a job.

There are pupils who have never mastered ligatures and retain a slow immature print. There are others who were not made sufficiently sure of their ligatures or convinced that cursive would be ultimately faster. They may well revert to print in secondary schools, and sadly teachers often encourage them to do so in the interest of legibility. Perhaps most disadvantaged of all is the quick-minded pupil who has evolved a personal shorthand with unrecognizable ligatures and subtractions, totally illegible to teachers and examiners alike. They need help, if only to show them how to retrain themselves.

This brings me to our last point – self-motivation. After a very young age, nothing concerning handwriting can be done against a child's own wishes. The exercises and sequences are virtually the same at 5 or 15, although the writing level and style obviously alters. Once the older pupils realize that they can learn the technique of developing repetitive exercises to cure their personal faults, a self-administered course works doubly well by removing the 'remedial' stigma and rebuilding confidence.

This book is just as relevant to the secondary school age group as the primary. It shows, on the one hand, what can go wrong from the start and why, and the results of poor teaching; and on the other, how good method could succeed and how remedial exercises can, at any age, help to right the faults.

2. Factors to consider before blaming a child for bad handwriting

The stroke-related remedial exercises that I suggest cannot, alone, cure deep-seated problems. May I make a plea to teachers at all levels before castigating a child for ill-formed or untidy, small or illegible handwriting, to think about the many factors that can be causing this. Certainly untidy handwriting should not be equated with low intelligence; it often indicates a mind moving too quickly for the hand, although an inability to form letters may be the result of some form of retardation. Bad handwriting may only be the symptom of deeper problems which need to be treated, or at any rate taken into consideration. Furthermore, undue criticism or unfeeling or uncomprehending pressure to improve handwriting may be counter-productive by adding to a child's tensions and worries.

First consider **physical reasons**: undetected or marginal physical handicaps causing poor coordination or limited movement, bad eyesight or deafness, severe left-handed problems, temporary ill health, overtiredness, or the effects of prescribed or even misused drugs, etc.

Then **psychological reasons**: undue tension caused by stress at home or at school from bereavement, a broken home, undue parental pressure to conform to an outward sign of progress, even a recent move of house can affect a child's writing; extreme shyness or introversion, resulting in lack of communication, probably written as well as verbal, etc.

Neurological reasons: cross laterality, or lack of left/right definition, or specific stroke problems sometimes due to otherwise unrelated brain damage or handicap, word-blindness, etc.

Environmental reasons: here one cannot separate school from home. The attitude to discipline, respect of people or skills, instilled by both parents and teachers, plus the prevailing atmosphere in home, classroom and society in general must also influence children's handwriting as an outward expression of their personality. Untidy homework may be the result of an underprivileged home with little privacy or space to write; but the attitudes of a home, rich or poor, are a more important influence. Lack of stimulation in children, left perhaps with baby-minders or elderly relatives, may result in learning difficulties and lack of concentration in the early years at school, affecting writing as well as other subjects.

Behavioural reasons: antagonism to a particular teacher, problems with other children including bullying or aggressiveness towards the whole educational system, will show in writing as well as the degree of interest that pupils have in the subject-matter they are writing about.

Teenagers' frequent changes of mood and developing character are often reflected in their confused, uneven and ever-changing hands. For better or worse, a child is even more likely to be influenced by an admired friend or teacher's hand than by the class model. Changes of fashion must be taken into account with sudden peer-group styles, as well as general experimentation on the part of an enquiring mind.

Stylistic reasons: inability to conform to an extreme model which is causing distortion of a child's natural hand, constant change of school and therefore models, resulting in a mixture of styles or possibly in confused and uneven writing: a teacher's personal preference for one letter form or another may cause unnecessary friction, and some of the unusual symbols used in the Initial Teaching Alphabet may continue to influence a child's later hand.

Lastly, in all fairness, consider whether the fault lies in poor teaching a child has received in the past, particularly by allowing stroke, grip and movement faults to remain undetected until they are so ingrained that they are difficult to eradicate. Take into account also the fact that lack of any strict skill-training during the formative years, in some modern education, not only deprives children of much satisfying and constructive achievement but means that they are starved of visual stimulation and awareness, leading to loss of critical faculties; nor do they develop adequate visual or aural memory – the very qualities needed to improve their handwriting.

However intangible the underlying problem or possibly difficult his behaviour, a child needs both informed help with his writing and understanding – and quite likely sympathy, too. A child with handwriting problems needs to be studied and treated individually.

Both of these examples are by the same 9-year-old girl. The school insisted on Marion Richardson writing but the child's natural hand was narrow and slanting. The resulting tension inhibited all written work and led to her having to change schools.

13

3. Practical factors to check before starting to write

These practical aspects are obviously most important during early training, but should be considered at any age or stage where writing difficulties are encountered.

Posture, seating and writing surface

Make sure that a child is comfortable and sitting straight on a chair that is suited to the height of the desk or table. Undoubtedly many older children work quite happily curled up in an armchair, or on the floor in front of the fire, but for those learning basic skills or with any problems, good posture and a satisfactory working surface are needed. Obviously, writing on a rough surface is going to cause trouble, but consider also that a smooth, hard table-top can be unsympathetic to write on when using a single sheet of paper. If a child is not using a notebook or pad, try a few thicknesses of scrap paper to make a nice resilient base, along the lines of an old-fashioned blotter.

Light

Make sure that there is sufficient light. Daylight or artificial light can cause as many problems as they solve if they are wrongly directed and cause the shadow of the writer's hand to obscure the work. Light should preferably come from the left side for the right-handed and the right side for the left-handers. This is easy enough to arrange at home but can cause problems in the classroom. Watch those children who naturally work with their heads bent over their books. Occasionally this is caused by poor vision and the child needs glasses; much more often the child has become used to writing in poor light.

Paper position

For a right-handed child the paper should be to the right of the line of the centre of the body, for the left-handed child to the left. This ensures free arm movement. Working with the arm across the body causes a cramped writing position and obscures the writer's view of the point of the implement. Paper can be at a slant as shown below:

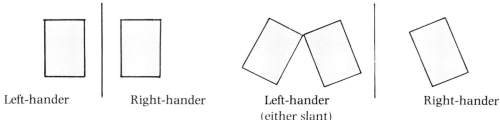

Left-hander   Right-hander   Left-hander   Right-hander

(either slant)

Everyone has an optimum writing position. This is the place where hand and pen are correctly positioned to work at their best. This obviously differs slightly from person to person. Adults tend to move large sheets of paper up and down and sometimes from side to side as they work, but you cannot expect a young child to do this. To make sure that the writing arm is neither unduly stretched or cramped, I suggest using small sheets of paper for both pre-writing skill training and pattern as well as for actual writing in class.

Writing implement

Both the point and barrel of the implement should suit the child, so provide a choice of pencils and pens in the classroom from thin fibre-tipped refills to fat pencils. You will soon notice which implement each child finds easiest to handle. Fat pencils sometimes add to the problems when infants are trying to establish an efficient pen hold; ordinary-sized pencils seem better for small hands. Pencil leads should not be too hard as sharp points tend to dig into the paper – this affects left-handers even more than right-handers. Fibre-tipped pens usually flow more freely than pencils and are especially useful in remedial situations. Modern pens need to be held at a different angle to pencils if they are to work well. A selection should let all children find the implement that works best for them. Freedom to choose often promotes interest in writing and increases children's cooperation when problems need solving. When felt or fibre-tipped pens begin to wear out they should be discarded before they can affect the quality of handwriting.

Paper surface

For those with limited physical movement or severe flow problems it is worth considering the paper surface in conjunction with whatever implement is being used, to ensure the least possible surface tension. At the other extreme a shiny, highly sized paper can cause loss of control, especially with a fibre tip which tends to slide. Again it is a matter of trial and error, keeping an open mind and fitting implement and paper to individual tastes and needs.

Pencil or pen hold

A firm but relaxed grip is needed, with the implement held between thumb and index finger, resting against the middle finger. The shaft, or handle, should be roughly in line with the forearm, for both right- and left-handed writers. Some modern implements require a more upright pen position. Test for free finger movement by getting children to try the exercises on page 38 and *watch* their hands. Individual help and demonstration when children first enter school can save a lot of problems later on.

Lines

This subject rouses strong feelings, and as so often it is the children that suffer from unbending rules. While it is accepted that many early lessons in pattern and letters are best on unlined paper, some children profit from at least a base line. Double lines and even four lines may well be helpful in certain circumstances to help overcome difficulties. Lines in exercise books should not be too close together so that older children are forced to write too small.

Double lines

Can be used to help a child to enlarge small writing or reduce large writing. The spacing of double lines should be chosen so as to suit the child's needs. The thickness of the point of the implement must also be taken into consideration to allow sensibly proportioned letters. One solution is to use blank exercise books and variably spaced ruling sheets to place under the pages.

4. The problem of left-handedness

Left-handed children have special problems that arise from dealing with an alphabet and writing designed for a right-handed world. However, if they are taught correctly from the beginning there is no reason why they should not develop as flowing a writing as any right-hander. The early lessons are the most important. If children are left unattended when they start school they often try to copy, or mirror, a neighbouring right-handed child's pencil hold. This awkward grip, once established, is extremely difficult to alter, and it is even considered by some experts harmful to try to do so. At the risk of being slightly repetitive, in addition to the general rules shown in the previous section, I would like to list the specific needs of left-handers.

Writing, paper position and light

In order to adopt a comfortable writing position with free arm movement for a left-hander, the paper must be placed to the left of the centre of the line of the body as shown on page 14. This will mean that the child must sit towards the right-hand side of a desk to leave enough space for the paper and books as well as elbow room. Children are sensible and logical: if the need for adequate light coming from the opposite side for their right-handed neighbours is explained and demonstrated to them, most likely they will sort this out for themselves, realizing the advantage of seeing their work clearly. They can organize it individually in the small informal groups and tables that are usually found in infant schools. In a formal classroom setting, with fixed seating, it is the teacher's responsibility to solve this problem.

kee P th at b oo k t idy

keep that book tidy

This left-hander could not see what she was doing. With a better position, pencil held higher up and sitting in better light, her letter spacing improved.

Writing implement and pen hold

A free flowing implement is especially important to left-handers as the direction of the movement of the pen is towards its point. Soft pencil leads do not dig into the paper as much as hard ones. If a left-hander has to use a traditional pen there are specially angled nibs, but a fibre-tipped pen may be a better choice. Find one that works at a suitable angle for the writer and remember that if the pen or pencil is held too close to the point the child cannot see what is being written. The relaxing scribble exercises are important for all ages as left-handers tend to grip their pens very tightly. A pen hold must work well for the writer. Some left-handers develop a twisted or 'inverted' hand position. This can happen when children cannot see what they are doing because paper is placed 'straight in front' or chairs are too low. An inverted pen hold can slow you down or become painful under pressure of speed. Writing on a blackboard (or whiteboard) gives young children practise in bringing the hand below the line of writing. Older pupils may need help to find a comfortable combination of paper position, hand position and pen hold.

Hand below the line

Hand above the line

Alternative penhold

The alternative pen hold works well for left- and right-handers and relieves tension. It lets modern pens find the best angle for writing.

5. The special writing problems of handicapped children

This is rather a specialized subject for a general book, but I would like to discuss some of the most relevant points, which are additional to those in the general section. It is even more important to consider each child's problems in the light of individual handicaps. With deformity of posture or limited physical movement, a comfortable writing position giving free arm movement may be impossible. Therefore teacher and child together will have to work out an optimum writing position. Where to put the paper, a free-flowing implement and suitable paper surface all become doubly important. In the case of a child with only one good hand, it may be necessary to fasten the paper to the writing surface to stop it slipping. Then the teacher must remember to move it from time to time.

It is tiring to sit in an awkward position to write, so sessions should be short. Many mentally as well as physically handicapped children can only concentrate for short periods, and any concerted physical or mental effort may wear them out.

Many handicaps result in poor posture, and this means that the teacher must consider the line of vision from eye to hand to ensure that the dominant eye is being used. Some children might have deformities which restrict or prevent the use of their natural writing arm. Both these circumstances can cause problems of laterality. The slant of the writing surface must be considered. Quite a steep slant can be helpful. As the height of the writing surface that suits one handicapped child may not suit another, the individual child should be allowed to experiment.

There is a range of pencils and fibre tips from narrowest refills to extra thick implements which should be available to teachers and parents. We have discussed young children's preferences for narrower handles. These may be of great assistance to some children with hand deformities, others may need just the opposite. An immobile hand can profit from a lump of plaster, polystyrene or even a ping-pong ball around the fattest pencil. These aids can, of course, be used to help adults as well as children.

Some handicapped children and some left-handers, or children with poor coordination, have special problems with the formation of certain strokes. The diagonal strokes are most likely to be troublesome. This is quite simple to test by using the patterns on the diagnostic card on page 40. Exercises may help, but if this is a permanent condition, writing can be made easier by using an alphabet with rounded v w y x and even z. This requires only a little knowledge of writing styles and letter forms. Children may find it fun to design an alphabet for themselves.

18

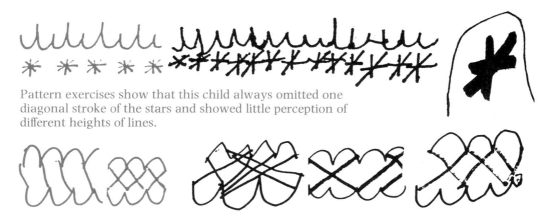

Pattern exercises show that this child always omitted one diagonal stroke of the stars and showed little perception of different heights of lines.

So much of a handicapped child's life and work is a direct challenge. Motivation and inventiveness can be harnessed to advantage in handwriting. In cases where it is within the child's capability, copy-book repetition and self-criticism can be rewarding, and the exercise of writing may help to improve manual dexterity. For those with more severe difficulties there is the alternative of using a typewriter. The more academic child may well be able to use handwriting in the earlier stages, but benefit from a typewriter later on, when longer passages such as essays might otherwise prove too tiring.

The relaxing and warming-up exercises on page 38 will be useful for regulating pressure and grip.

Handicapped children will profit more than most from demonstration with their own implement on their own paper. Then they can be helped to copy and adapt pencil hold and pattern or letter movement to their own needs. Pictorial aids such as those on page 41 or verbal description of movement such as 'down up and over' for a letter n or similes such as 'down like falling rain', are especially helpful to those less able to move themselves. In tackling the wide variety of problems facing handicapped children, teacher and child will need to use exceptional initiative.

A village street made of 5-year-olds' interpretations of the corrective pattern for h; one of the pictorial aids that I developed at the suggestion of a teacher of handicapped children.

6. Comparison of current teaching styles

Teachers and parents need to be able to compare various handwriting styles and schemes in use in our schools today. Then they might be able to understand why so many children are confused and be better able to deal with ensuing problems. There is, for better or worse, no official directive on style; more unfortunate, there is no accepted method of teaching handwriting either nationally or regionally. There is seldom co-operation between separate infant and junior schools, much less between junior and secondary schools within a district. Even within many schools there can be confusion.

Where there is no policy on the teaching of handwriting, individual teachers teach their own preferred letter forms. This can result in children having to learn three different styles in three consecutive years with disastrous results. At the other extreme, the school model may be rigorously enforced with little or no consideration of the personal factors that influence children's writing nor the plight of children moving from school to school. Some head-teachers are totally committed to one style or another and are themselves good teachers and exponents of it, but other teachers in the school are seldom as capable.

This boy had been taught three different styles in consecutive years. Some letters were round and upright; some sloped forward, and his **f** backwards. First he had to choose an angle, then design himself an alphabet.

There is often no real understanding of a model's purpose. In trying to make children copy a frequently distorted letter-form, teachers forget the movement and flow of writing, which is of primary importance. The children's point of view and the long-term benefit for them seems seldom considered. So what can be done about this? Teachers must understand the principles behind the main teaching styles. Each has been carefully designed with a slightly different purpose in mind, although all teach the same alphabet and roughly the same writing movement. Writing is a personal matter, and in my view each of these styles has its good and bad points. Of course teachers can use their own letters, and this can, if pursued methodically, be successful, especially in the early stages. They must, however, be aware of what movement for better or worse they are training into the child at an impressionable age. (I refer here particularly to entry strokes which are explained on page 31.) Equally important, whether using a model or their own letters, teachers must be consistent in writing on the blackboard, in display, and in all teaching material.

Italic handwriting

There are several schemes aimed at teaching italic writing to schoolchildren. These letter forms, which are based on sixteenth-century writing, are perhaps the most beautiful of all; they should lead to a graceful, compressed slanting hand which is both fluent and economical in line. Most of the systems have a simplified first alphabet. Unfortunately most of these are static, without joining strokes at the base, and however well-designed their letters may be, children will have trouble retraining to a flowing writing movement.

I am all in favour of encouraging pupils in secondary schools who are attracted to this style to learn it. They will have an established movement by then, and distinctive tastes. However I am not at all convinced that it is ideal for young children.

Italic handwriting should only be taught by well-trained teachers. Far too often it is distorted into a tortuous pointed hand in primary schools, or becomes an illegible zig-zag when speeded up. The discipline of a broad-edged nib, on which these schemes so often hinge, is helpful to some children. When everyone is made to use an italic pen, there are unlucky children who find it an unsuitable writing implement and have a difficult time. If it is not used at the correct angle of 45° the balance of the letters is wrong. Left-handers, even with specially angled pens, can find this a problem. A broad-edged nib can slow down and distort the writing of children whose natural inclination is towards a rounder hand, and who are already struggling with an unsuitable model. The rigidity of the pen can make the speeding-up of italic writing difficult even if a good letter has been taught. Some of the excellent work shown by primary schools is more like formal lettering than handwriting, and little thought is given to the speed that will be required in secondary school. Only those with a natural inclination towards italic writing will overcome this problem. Others will have to struggle to develop a natural fast writing hand on their own. There is little time and even less help once they leave junior school.

A good letter is a good letter regardless of the implement used. Italic letter forms, in the widest sense, can be written with modern implements too, and a less jagged letter often results.

Those very adults who love and understand beautiful letters may, in their wish to let children have the aesthetically best model, actually be doing harm by exposing them to it too young.

An 18-year-old's flowing italic, developed from an admired master's hand.

responsibility for the results of their deeds should not fall on any one of them individually.

Italic teaching hands

nnnnnnnnnn
nhnhnhnhn

From Charlotte Stone and Alfred Fairbank: *Beacon Writing Book One*
(Ginn and Company Limited).

in din nun imp him did
pen at cup kin emu emu

From *Platignum Italic Booklet*.

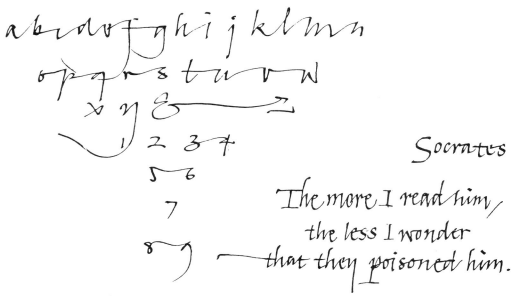

a b c d e f g h i j k l m n
o p q r s t u v w
x y z

1 2 3 4
5 6
7
8

Socrates

The more I read him,
the less I wonder
that they poisoned him.

A freely written alphabet that demonstrates the seldom seen possibilities of italic as a
fast personal hand. Example of very quickly written italic with formal qualities.
Both by Gunnlaugur S E Briem.

Primary school children's italic writing, distorting the model.

used along wet-work wives
was beheaded born some time
Beautiful expensive people

Taught like this the italic influence seldom lasts or benefits young children.

pencil

Heavens little woodworm
You've eaten all the chairs

broad-edged nib

I had an accident when i ran down
the hill to the shop to get the groceries I

ball point

Club. For the organised game we
did High Jump and Long Jump

Pupils who learn this hand at a later age (14–15) often go on to develop a fast, interesting adult italic-based writing such as the example shown below.

C.H. at
15 years

There weren't really any difficulties about The measuring,
apart from the rats! Some interesting facts were revealed.
Unfortunately I do not know The address or even The name

C.H. at
18 years

heavy clouds and late summer
sunshine. I rose at seven and went
out to sketch The Market Cross
I saw a lovely church at Loddon

C.H. at
23 years

I didn't expect your envelope to
contain anything so considerable as
an etching by Killon, and although
I am familiar with his work, I felt

The Marion Richardson system

Marion Richardson writing is based on patterns developed from children's natural movements. It has been in use for fifty years and is still popular in many British schools. Children as young as 5 or 6 years old, taught by her method, can write a clear, round cursive hand. However, pattern must be taught as carefully as letters. Unless the correct point of entry and direction of stroke is used, the pattern exercises are useless and even harmful. This pattern *ℓℓℓ* seems to encourage *ℓ*. Some of the patterns bear little relation to actual letters; otherwise I am broadly in favour of this method for very young children. It is the letter forms themselves that are at fault. The movements that Marion Richardson found natural in young children lead to a round letter, which in turn means an uneconomic cursive and later on an immature-looking hand. By oversimplifying the letters to encourage that early flow, some unattractive characters are formed. The letter **p** is the worst of all. Both the open **p** and **b** deteriorate when speeded up, and with personal subtractions and ligatures sometimes end up as a simple upright. By 8 years old at the latest, children need to be helped to modify these letters. They should be shown the advantages of a narrow letter, and how slanting it makes joining up easier and quicker. Then at least they have a choice. They should be shown a closed **p** and **b** and the alternatives for **v**, **w** and **x** and for both double and single **s**, and **f**, and then they will be able to develop a more mature-looking hand.

From Marion Richarson: *Writing and Writing Patterns Book Two* (Hodder and Stoughton).

A swarm of bees in July
Is not worth a fly.

This is an example of a 6-year-old's work.

Mark

the Nile begins , a long way
from most of the farms . Dams
have been built to stop some

But, by the age of 8, children should be taught to narrow their letters.

My class and I are very
grateful to you for letting us see
about the house and showing us
your balcony and the bedroom and
ever other place.

This 9-year-old has narrowed her letters but has not been shown how to change her **b**s
and **p**s.

past bad by impossible king

If the open **b** and **p** are not altered they deteriorate at speed. Secondary school children
show the **b** losing its bowl until it becomes confused with an **l**.

Changing priorities around the world

Fashions in handwriting models are always changing. Some countries have national models which they have not altered for a century or more, while others alter them regularly and sometimes dramatically, in the hope of improving handwriting in their schools. The emphasis is now on models for infants which train the hand in the right movement and pressure to lead quickly to relaxed joined letters. Many countries are moving away from static print script letters for infants. The fact that some of the illustrations in this book show letters without exit strokes does not mean that I approve of print script. Now that speed is such a priority, economical letters with integral exit strokes on the baseline are becoming more popular whatever the style, slant or proportion of the model. The old fashioned continuous cursives are gradually being phased out as being inefficient and unsuitable for modern pens. On the opposite page you can see the letterforms that have now replaced the copperplate-based models in many Australian states, and on page 29, the models that are beginning to replace looped cursives in the USA.

The influence of computers

The increasing use of computers in schools has made everyone think more seriously about the usage of handwriting. Some tasks may be better performed with the help of modern technology. Handwriting is no longer the universal means of communication that it was a century ago. Our hands were not developed to undergo the strain of long periods of writing legibly at speed, under the kind of pressure that faces the best of our students today. The more personal tasks, such as note taking, are the functions that are best performed by hand, and it is towards the needs of these tasks that we should direct our teaching today. The handwritten letter, expressing the personality of the writer before you even start to read it, will also survive, maybe heralding a renaissance in the more aesthetic aspects of the written word. Finished project work and secondary school essays, however, may well be better presented on the computer. This is not an excuse for saying that handwriting need no longer be taught in primary schools. It is all a matter of finding a sensible balance - not forgetting that mastery of the keyboard is a skill in itself that takes up teaching time and needs a lot of practice to become fast enough to be a useful everyday tool of communication in mainstream education.

This is how you should view the more modern models on the following pages. Judge for yourself those which would lead to a fast, efficient, legible and above all a flexible enough personal handwriting to enable the writer to tackle the variety of tasks that will need to be faced.

Basic modern hands

a b c d e f g h i j k l m n
o p q r s t u v w x y z

Stage Two,
hooks added
prior to joining

a b c d e f g h i j k l m n
o p q r s t u v w x y z

Stage Three,
joined where
appropriate
only

abcdefghijklmn
opqrstuvwxyz

From Christopher Jarman: *The Development of Handwriting Skills* (Simon and Schuster).

A B C D Ð E F G a b c d ð e f g
H I J K L M N h i j k l m n o
O P Q R S T U V p q r s t u v w
W X Y Z Þ Æ Ö x y z þ œ ö

An italic alphabet by Gunnlaugur S E Briem from his handwriting scheme for Iceland.

abcdefghijklmn opqrstuvwxyz

abcdefghijklmn opqrsstuvwxyz

- The foundations of joined handwriting
- Developing automatic handwriting

The Victorian Infant Cursive and Modern Cursive, used in several Australian states.

Excerpts from other teaching manuals

knock at the door,

Chat with a chimp.

From *New Nelson Handwriting*, by Peter Smith (Thomas Nelson and Sons Ltd).

abcdefghijklmnopqrstuvwxyz

From *Write away*, devised by Tom Barnard (Philip and Tacey).

	small letters	capital letters
Group 1 **Downstrokes**	iltujy	ILTJHEU
Group 2 **Clockwise**	rnmhbpk	DBPR
Group 3 **Anticlockwise**	cadgqoe	OQCG
Group 4 **Diagonals**	vwxz	AKVWNMXYZ
Group 5 **Direction changers**	sf	SF

From *Ginn Handwriting*. This uses Sassoon Primary script and joined script as a model.

Handwriting models from the USA

In the United States there is, as yet, no concensus for a change in the national model which has been in use for more than a century. Italic hands, such as the one illustrated here, and other simplified models, are making considerable inroads into the looped commercial cursive strongholds. In practice, the handwriting of young Americans is becoming as varied and personal as that in Great Britain, as the discipline is relaxed, and it is realised that copperplate-based continuous cursives fall apart when written at speed and strain the hand because there are no penlifts. Older students need to adapt to a more economical and less painful way of writing, but unless something is done soon to meet their needs, they will turn away from handwriting altogether and use computers instead.

D'Nealian™ Manuscript

a b c d e f g h i j k l m n
o p q r s t u v w x y z

D'Nealian™ Cursive

a b c d e f g h i j
k l m n o p q r
s t u v w x y z

From *D'Nelian Handwriting* (Scott, Foresman and Company).

Undercurve beginnings, minimum letters.	i u w e r s
Intermediate letters.	t d p itl
Undercurve beginnings, upper-loop letters.	l b f h k
Overcurve beginnings, hump-letters.	n m v x y z
Downcurve beginnings, small oval group.	a d g q o c
Lower-loop letters.	f q p y z z f
Check-stroke letters.	r b o w s s

Zaner-Bloser Commercial Cursive Alphabet.

When learning manuscript and commercial cursive,

animal   animal
this   becomes   this

When learning Italic,

animal   animal
this   becomes   this

From Denys Taipale: *Italic Handwriting Manual.* This detailed writing programme is particularly well-suited to the American educational system.

Initial teaching alphabet

The Initial Teaching Alphabet is no longer as popular as it once was. It was designed to help children in the early stages of reading and spelling but can cause problems that show up in handwriting at a later stage. It may be relatively easy for children to transfer to reading and spelling with traditional orthography but results of early handwriting training by the I.T.A. method can be seen in many teenagers' handwriting today. The I.T.A. symbols are purposely tied to print and were not designed to join up; some of them have movements counter to the normal letters that have to be relearned. This is going to make it even more difficult for children to develop a natural cursive hand.

apple chair eel king book food ship treasure mother is

Alphabets in general

Broadly speaking, any of these alphabets, with the exception of I.T.A., if they are intelligently, consistently and tolerantly taught, will benefit a child.

By **intelligently** I mean using the alphabet and method for the good of the child at the right stage of development. I also mean that its advantages should be understood and used, and that the teacher should watch out for the faults arising out of each system's shortcomings.

By **consistently** I mean not causing confusion to children. If a school has chosen a style, then all teachers there should endeavour to master it, and use it at all times. Writing is such a personal matter that certain letters, or even the principle behind an alphabet, may offend some teachers or parents. Whenever possible, in the first couple of years at school, it is probably best for parents to be told, or even instructed, in the system being used. Then they can be asked not to confuse children by voicing their objections to them. Sometimes when looking at the scheme as a whole, parents object to what is only a temporary stage in the long-term writing programme. If what is being taught is really harming a child then of course I will support any concerned parent's complaint. This brings me to my third point:

By **tolerantly** I mean that a school should allow any child, however young, who patently cannot manage the prescribed style or implement, to change to something that suits the individual need. Certainly, by the age of 8, any child who has learned the correct movement should be helped to add or subtract from the model and develop a personal cursive. A model is an aid to be used only as long as it is necessary before being discarded.

7. Priorities when choosing a school model

When choosing a style for use as a school model, various things are considered, from the head teacher's personal inclinations to the price of teaching aids. Before making a final choice for a primary school, the head teacher should look at the work of secondary school children, not necessarily in his own area, so as to assess the results and shortcomings of the various teaching styles and methods which are usually easily visible.

My priorities for a model

(1) A flowing first alphabet that leads naturally into cursive. Separate letters with joining strokes are quite within the capabilities of 5-year-olds.

(2) Although rounded letters may be easier to write and recognize at 5 years old, perfectly rounded letters are less easy to join up, so the advantages of a slightly narrowed letter from the start should be considered. Any second alphabet should have its letters based on an oval and preferably have a slight forward slant. This leads to a more economical style and easier joins to the round family of letters.

(3) Emphasis on the exit stroke, not the entry stroke. This is rather difficult to explain. There is nothing wrong with an entry stroke in itself; in some ways it is an assistance in initiating flow and indicating a point of entry. It is more a matter of how it is taught and allowed to develop. By teaching either _n_ or _n_ the teacher is training a definite movement which will be difficult to alter. The first entry stroke _n_ is good as long as it is kept neat and small, and it is always shown that the exit stroke of the first letter joins the entry stroke of the second letter. Far too often entry strokes are exaggerated. They may have become a cover for hesitation or an excuse for ornamentation. Then letters overlap with no flow at all. The second entry stroke above is based on copperplate movement, which originally had a thick downstroke and thin upstroke.

Beware of disobliging your parents, or teachers
Joseph Wilkes December 8th 1840.

When this combination of join and entry stroke is used more heavily, the two can deteriorate to give the appearance of an extra i between letters.

(4) A flexible model that would enable a child to develop a personal style. If a model depends on a broad-tipped nib for training, then it should demonstrate also how the same letters can be written with other implements. This is really moving to my next point: How I judge a teaching system or programme. Here my priorities would be:

(a) Clear practical instruction on such subjects as paper position and pencil grip, with a logical explanation for the rules and possible alternatives. Most of the manuals that I have seen express strong and sometimes contradictory views on paper position. Some are quite incorrect. Few mention the different angles needed for different writing implements or the need for experimentation to find the conditions appropriate to an individual child, particularly a left-hander.

(b) A progressive system which is not only pattern-based at 5 years old but uses pattern for exercise and correction throughout.

(c) A system where letters are taught from the beginning in stroke-related families, not alphabetically, which aids movement irrespective of style.

I am not in favour of the introduction of a national teaching hand which, however well researched, assumes a right and a wrong in a subject that is so personal.

A round and upright style, or one that is narrow and slanting, will always be contrary to the character and natural inclination of a proportion of any group. Teachers trained in the basics of letter forms can deal knowledgeably and flexibly with each child.

That is why I advocate that during the last two years of primary school children should be actively encouraged to break away from any model. They may need help redesigning their writing, especially with such combinations as **ss** and **ff**, and would profit from looking at different adult forms of handwriting.

Letting children develop freely a fast personal hand would avoid the tension that can arise between teacher and pupil, and the frustration often felt by older children whose writing is being forced into an unnatural mould.

It should also help those whose otherwise close adherence to an extreme model may be inhibiting the speeding up of their writing. These are the children whose writing is most likely to deteriorate rapidly when they are forced to write faster in secondary schools.

Cooperation between junior and secondary schools is advantageous to all concerned.

8. Typefaces that 5-year-olds may encounter

	1	2	3	4	5
Group 1	i l	i l	i l	i l	i l
	t u	t u	t u	t u	t u
	y j	y i	y j	y j	y j
Group 2	m n	m n	m n	m n	m n
	r h	r h	r h	r h	r h
	b p	b p	b p	b p	b p
	k	k	k	k	k
Group 3	c a	c a	c a	c a	c a
	d g	d g	d g	d g	d g
	q o	q o	q o	q o	q o
	e	e	e	e	e
Group 4	s f	s f	s f	s f	s f
	v w	v w	v w	v w	v w
	x z	x z	x z	x z	x z

Typefaces similar to numbers 2-5 are found in reading books for young children but some of the letterforms would conflict with your handwriting policy. The typeface in column 1, Sassoon Primary. is specially designed to be legible and conform to most of the principles of handwritten letters.

33

9. Stroke-related letter families

Letters should be taught and corrected in stroke-related families, not alphabetically. Repeating and comparing similar strokes and letters reinforce the correct writing movement.

If we use flowing separate letters as a first alphabet, the letter families will be:

(1) **itluyj**   line and anti-clockwise arch

(2) **nmrh bpk**   line and clockwise arch

(3) **cadgqoe**   anti-clockwise circular letters

(4) **sf vwxz**   *f* and letters with diagonal strokes.

Certain letters will have to change groups if a different model is used.

If **y** is taught as **y** then it joins **v w x z** in group (4).

Likewise **k** , if it is taught as **k**

If **b** is taught as **ʊ** then it would be in a group (1) with rounded **ʊ** and **ɯ** if these are taught instead of **v** and **w** .

In most alphabets there are one or two letters which do not fit into any group. In this case they are **s** and **f** .

This is not a copy book; my own letters are not a model to copy exactly and are purposely kept as neutral as possible. They stress movement rather than neatness or style. As shown by some later illustrations I may have to conform with the school model to avoid confusion.

All the exercises are meant to be copied by the teacher into the class model. The point of entry and direction of stroke should be indicated in whatever way the school chooses. This should be consistent.

Some ways of indicating point of entry and direction of stroke.

10. Capital letters

As capital letters and numerals are not meant to join up, the sequencing of the strokes and the point of entry are, to my mind, less important than with small letters. Take the capital letter **M**. It can equally correctly be sequenced starting from top left-hand corner downwards as most small letters do, or from bottom left corner upwards resulting in the letter being written in one continuous movement. The same is true of **A** and **N**.

These three different ways of constructing **M** are taught in three current teaching manuals.

Of course it will be necessary to teach and demonstrate capital letters to young children. They are as likely to be a teacher's own letters as those from a manual. Even if they are supposedly from a manual, I would guess that the teacher's own accustomed sequencing will often prevail over a strange one, so strong is the sequencing habit of a lifetime.

The letters must be recognizable and some sequencing, such as these early **T**s, would obviously have to be corrected. Children who have developed perfectly reasonable but differently sequenced capital letters from the preferred ones of their teacher should not be made to change.

I can see little point in teaching children the proportions of capital letters, though some manuals still do. If extra teaching or remedial help is needed, capital letters can be arranged in stroke-related families. The letters below are not intended to be used as a model.

ILT F E H UJ   line and arch

COQGD B R P   circular

ANMVWYKXZ S   diagonal

11. Numerals

Similar differences occur in the teaching of numerals. There is not much argument about how to write **1** and **2**. **3** can have a flat or rounded top 3 or 3 . **4** appears in several different styles, closed 4 or open 4 4 . With **5** there are two separate approved points of entry 5 and 5 ; the first one can deteriorate to resemble a letter **s**. Whatever the books say, the number **8** has several points of entry and adults write it equally legibly in both directions, 8 or the more usual 8 . The preferred shape for a **9** is 9 because teachers consider it the most legible form. However, **9** is really a reversal of **6** and some children use, whether they are taught it or not, the more logical but less legible 9 .

So, once again, I would say that a school should be consistent in demonstrating and teaching its preferred numerals but not try to change a child who has learned or developed a perfectly legible alternative sequencing or style of number.

Numerals for children should be all the same size and written so that their tops and bases are in line. In lettering, typography and adult hands, different levels are sometimes used.

It might be a help to have a chart of printed numerals of the various typefaces used in the different mathematical programmes to compare with the numerals written in class.

1	2	3	4	5	6	7	8	9	0
1	2	3	4	5	6	7	8	9	0
1	2	3	4	5	6	7	8	9	0
1	2	3	4	5	6	7	8	9	0
1	2	3	4	5	6	7	8	9	0

Typographically numerals vary less than letters and children are seldom confused.

12. Explaining the stroke-related system

The system I have devised should be easy to understand and use.
Pattern, separate letters and cursive are the operative stages.
Pattern is subdivided into:

(1) Exercises for free finger movement
(2) Exercises for pencil control
(3) Exercises for separate directional strokes
(4) Exercises to teach or correct a specific letter or group of letters

The stages of writing referred to are

nmrh   nmrh bpk   nmhr
static print   flowing separate letters   cursive

By static I refer to the lack of any joining strokes at the base of even
the single-stroke letters i and l and t. This does not infer static
construction. However plain the print, it must be constructed in such a
way that the pencil is not lifted while writing a letter (except for dots and
cross-strokes and the letter x) and that it finishes in such a position that
logical joining strokes can follow naturally. A simple first alphabet
should have joining strokes at the base of letters iltunmha
and d leading naturally to the easiest sets of ligatures.

Cursive can eventually be divided into the simple school-taught style
with regular ligatures, and the faster, more adult one with increasingly
personal characteristics and ligatures.

When teachers isolate a particular stroke or letter problem, which is
often more easily detected by watching children write than from finished
written work, they should initially revert to a previous stage - from
cursive to separate letter or separate letter to pattern. It may be desirable
to clarify by slightly enlarging the work, perhaps using a larger
pointed implement. Practise the necessary stage of relevant pattern,
graded stroke or letter sequence, then words until the correct movement
is established.

The longer the problem has been neglected, the longer it will take to
cure.

These exercises are aimed at correcting the formation of letters, so
they cannot alone be expected to cure deep-seated or multiple learning
difficulties, but they may sort out some of the simpler problems without
adding to the child's confusion.

13. The stages of pattern: 1

Exercises to ensure free finger movement, for use with beginners or at any time to relax a tense grip

Stage 2

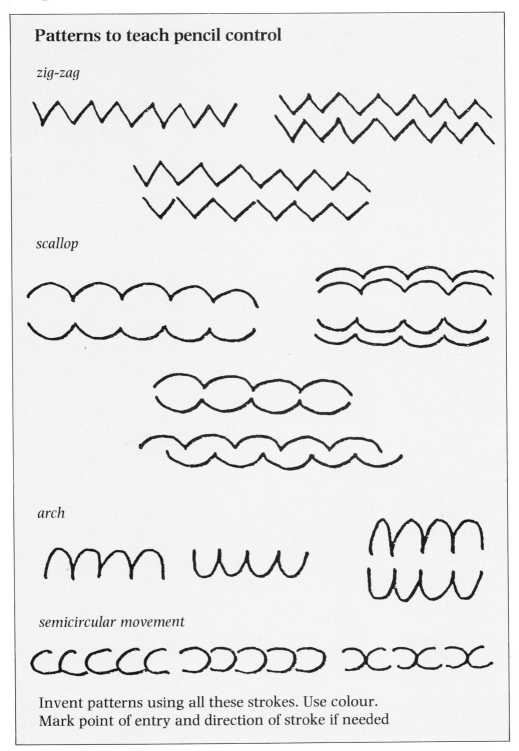

Patterns to teach pencil control

zig-zag

scallop

arch

semicircular movement

Invent patterns using all these strokes. Use colour.
Mark point of entry and direction of stroke if needed

Stage 3

Can be used for diagnostic purposes as it includes all directional strokes

Patterns to teach vertical and horizontal strokes

||| ≡ ||| ≡ ||| # # #

+ | + | + | + | + | + | + |

To teach diagonal strokes

/// \\\ /// \\\   ⟪⟪⟨◊⟩⟫⟫   ⋀⋀⋀⋀

+ X + X + X + X   ✳ ✳ ✳ ✳ ✳ ✳

To teach ascending and descending strokes

short stroke and ascender   short stroke and descender

ı|ı|ı|ı|ı|ı|ı| '|'|'|'|'|'|'|'

both together   ı|ı|ı|ı|ı|ı

ı|ı|ı|ı|ı|ı|ı| ı|'|'|'|'|'|'

Curves with uprights, anti-clockwise or clockwise

ı c ı c ı c ı c ı c ı c   ı ɔ ı ɔ ı ɔ ı ɔ ı ɔ ı

with ascender or descender

c|c|c| c|c|c| |ɔ|ɔ|ɔ |ɔ|ɔ|ɔ|
both together

c|c|c|c|c|c|c |ɔ|ɔ|ɔ|ɔ|ɔ|ɔ

Complete circles with uprights are easier but teach and reveal less

o|o|o|o o|o|o|o o|o|o|o o|o|o|o|

40

Stage 4

Patterns to teach or correct a specific letter or letter group

letter group	pattern	pictorial aid
¹ itluyj	uy uu using letter shapes	 umbrella
2a nmrh	hm m	 house or huts
Line and arch letters from groups 1 and 2a	hm uy hm uy	
2b hbpk	hm hm mm mm or hm pm	
³ cadgqoe	ccco ccca or cccd cccg	 caterpillar
⁴ sf vwxz		 swan
For point of entry	c s c s f sc f sc	
Superimpose **V** and **W** on a narrow zig-zag	wwww vwvw	
X and **Z** on a wider zig-zag	www zxx	

41

14. Layouts for practice cards

```
i . . . . . . . . . . . . . . . .
i . l . . . . . . . . . . . .
i . . t . . . . . . . . . . .
i . . u . . . . . . . . .
u . . y . . . . . . . .
y . . j . . . . . . . .
```

```
i l t u y j
. . . . . . . . . . . . . . . . . .
i l t u y j
. . . . . . . . . . . . . . . . . .
i l t u y j
. . . . . . . . . . . . . . . . . .
```

Copy these progressive stroke-related sequences into the school model. Mark the point of entry and direction of stroke, if necessary.

```
n . . . . . . . . . . . . . . .
n . . . m . . . . . . . .
n . . . r . . . . . . . .
n . . . h . . . . . . . .
h . . . b . . . . . . . .
b . . . p . . . . . . . .
b . . . k . . . . . . . .
```

```
n m r h b p k
. . . . . . . . . . . . . . . . . .
n m r h b p k
. . . . . . . . . . . . . . . . . .
n m r h b p k
. . . . . . . . . . . . . . . . . .
```

c ....
c ... a ....
a ... d ....
a ... g ....
a ... q ....
c ... o ....
c ... e ....

c a d g q o e

....

c a d g q o e

....

c a d g q o e

....

The teaching letter for each group comes first. It is repeated, then teaches the next letter. The horizontal layout repeats the whole family.

s ....
s ... f ....
v ....
v ... w ....
x ....
x ... z ....

s f v w x z

....

s f v w x z

....

s f v w x z

....

15. Teaching and remedial exercises explained in letter families

Line and arch letters are the easiest to learn and should be tackled first. For repetitive exercises I suggest combining families (1) and (2). Both are needed to form simple words and their problems are similar.

Letter family (1)   *iltuyj*

Letter family (2)   *nmrh bpk*

The relevant early patterns for teaching or correcting those letters are:

(1) To relax grip

(2) To learn control and movement   isolate a letter

(3) To learn ascending and descending strokes

b p and *k* may need

In this system there is a key teaching letter which is the easiest to write in each family. In family (1), once the downward movement of an *i* is learned, it is repeated in *l t* and *u*. When *u* is formed correctly it leads on to *y*. The last stroke of the *y* is echoed by the *j*. In family (2) *n* teaches *m r* and *h*; *h* leads on to *b p* and *k*.

There is thus a key remedial letter which helps to correct the most usual faults in each family. Sometimes the same letter is used both to teach and correct.

Correcting letter faults in families 1 and 2

With young children the most usual faults when writing the letters in families (1) and (2) are:

(1)   (2)   (3)

No final or initial stabilizing stroke. This makes it impossible for letters to join up.

No flowing movement whether the correct point of entry is used or not.

44

| (4) | (5) | (6) |

Descenders wrongly formed.

Wrong point of entry, direction of stroke or right-to-left construction make it impossible to join up these letters later on.

The letter to correct fault (1) is y. Providing the y is correctly written the sequence yuyuyu accentuates the necessary final downstroke and corrects the u. The letter to correct fault (2) is h. Providing the h is correctly written the sequence hnhnhn accentuates the necessary initial downstroke and corrects the n then m or r.

Children with fault (1) often have fault (2) as well. This can be the result of quick-minded children getting impatient with static print and trying to speed up their writing. It must be dealt with as soon as it appears or children will have great difficulty in changing their movement and developing a cursive.

Once the flowing movement has been described, demonstrated, and exercised with pattern uuuu mmm , then the letters to correct fault (3) are again y and h alternating with u and n. The letter to correct fault (4) is a well written u to correct the y in the sequence uyuy or uyjuyj yjyjyj or uyjuyj will help to correct a wrongly constructed j.

If these faults are caught early, it may be enough to repeat the key remedial letter in a simple sequence. If the fault recurs occasionally in children's creative writing, the key letter or short sequence can be used each time as a reminder.

If the faults are persistent, or as in numbers (5) and (6) involve a right-to-left movement, then a more positive letter pattern correction can be used.

For letter family (1)

For letter family (2)

If both families are involved

The repetitive pattern entry or exit emphasize the correct left-to-right movement, and will be extremely difficult to write in the reverse direction. I would like to stress that faults of point-of-entry or direction are less likely to occur with flowing separate letters than with static print. Each corrective letter pattern can be made into a pictorial reminder:

For family (1)   For family (2)

umbrella   hut or house

Some teachers like to put these corrective pictures at the top of the appropriate practice card. They were originally designed at the request of a teacher of handicapped children, but all young children seem to enjoy and remember them and they are a useful relaxation and reward at the end of a session.

Progressive repetitive letter and word sequences for families 1 and 2

Progressive stroke-related letter sequences and, later on, words and phrases, are useful to establish flow and movement and to reinforce both teaching and remedial work.

For those with multiple problems the letter sequences have an additional advantage. They remove the worry of spelling and allow children to concentrate solely on letter formation. Dots can be omitted to start with and the first set of sequences allows for flow to be established without the child having to worry about ascending or descending strokes.

static print	flowing separate letter	cursive
ı u ı u ı u ı u ı u no	ululululul	ininininin
ın ın ın ın ın dot	ınmınmın	ınmınmın
ınmınmın	ınrmınrm	unununu
ınumınum	ınumınum	unımunım
mini nun	rım run ruın	minimum

46

Notice that the sequences change with the different writing stages: whereas ininin is a logical reinforcement of movement in static print, it is not logical in flowing separate letters inin inin becomes just a running pattern in cursive. I have omitted r in the cursive sequence as it has a top join and the shape has to be changed from r to r The cursive sequence unun is useful in teaching the necessity of differentiating between the two arched curves. Sequences must be selected to suit individual problems. Some children may have special problems with ascending or descending strokes, some with perceiving letter height and some with just one letter.

These cursive sequences are those that I refer to throughout the book as simple flow exercises for relaxing tension and adjusting writing angle and ligatures.

static print   flowing separate letter

ililililil   ilitlitlitl   ililililil   ililitlitlit

uyuyuy   uyjuyjuy   uyuyuy   uyjuyju

iluyiluy   hnuyhnu   iluyiluy   hnuyhn

lit my hilly   hint runny try

cursive

ululululul   ululitlitl

uy uy uy u   uyj uyj uyj

uy uy uy uy   uy uy uy u

hnuyhnuy   uhnyuhny

hit hilly hymn tiny jilt

Stroke related phrases appear on page 53 in the section on spacing.

Exercises for letter family 3

The relevant early patterns for teaching and correcting these letters are:

(1) To relax and correct grip

(2) To learn control

(3) To alternate curves with ascenders and descenders

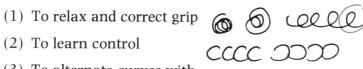

isolate a letter

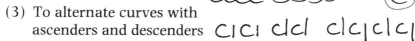

The key teaching letter is C. It teaches O and a. a teaches d and g.

The key remedial letter is also C, which corrects O and a.

Then either C or a corrects other letters.

The pictorial pattern is

caterpillar.

The most usual faults are:

(1)

ζC

resulting in

$\zeta a \, g \, d e$

(2)

$\swarrow C$

resulting in

$u \, v \, y$

(3)

$a g d d \quad o a g d$

no flow whether correct point of entry or not

The first two faults need the key letter C explained carefully, demonstrated and corrected first. The point of entry and direction of stroke must be clearly marked for the first faults, then the sequences cococo or cocacoca written so the teacher can see that the correct movement is established. Fault (2) needs a diagram such as c: or c:c:c: to explain the entry and shape of C.

The caterpillar helps too. Its body falls apart with a faulty C. The sequence chchch can be useful. Then a faulty C, such as in chchich, can be dotted to show that it has deteriorated to look like i. This is useful for older children whose cursive letters are poorly formed.

When the letter c is correct, the teaching and remedial sequences to reinforce the right movement and cure faults (1) (2) and (3) are:

ccco   ccca   cccd   cccg   and   cccq

then

ccco ccca	cocacoca	adadada
ccca cccd	cacdcacd	dgdgdg
ccca cccg	cacgcacg	adagad
cccg cccq	cgcqcgcq	qugaqug

words: add dad cad dog cod cog quad

The sequences ccco ccca cccd or words like cocoa are also helpful in spacing exercises, see page 53.

There are special problems with e and d because these two letters do not start at the top: ℮ ℮ d d etc. It must be carefully explained and demonstrated to children that these are middle-starting letters. e starts left to right then upwards. d starts right to left then downwards.

Superimposing e on eeeeeeee can help. The point of entry and direction must be marked e˄ d˄, letters practised separately, then sequences cecece or adadad should help, followed by words such as ace aged added dead.

Letter reversal

Letter reversal can be explained to some children with letter families. b and d are the letters most often involved in reversal. If b and d are sometimes confused but a correctly written, the sequence adadad and words add dad may help by visually tying the problem letter to one that is known in the same family. Likewise, if p is correctly written and only b confused, the sequence pbpbpb, leading to the word pub, may be a useful reminder. This helps only when there is visual confusion. Where the problem is phonetic or aural the opposite approach may help. Both letters may be shown together in the sequences bdbd pgpg, etc., then choosing words such as bed which has the advantage of a pictorial reminder |bed|, bad bid bud or peg pig pug even g‖a‖p.

Another way of tackling this problem that might help some children is to use less similar versions of the letters involved, e.g. ʅ and ∂ .

Exercises for letter family 4

This group consists of three pairs of letters which are not as closely related as the letters in the other families. **v, w, x** and **z** are made up of diagonal strokes. The relevant patterns for these letters are:

wide and narrow zig-zags

It may be useful for those who have problems with these letters to superimpose them on wide and narrow zig-zags.

Those who have real difficulty in controlling diagonal strokes can use alternatives for these letters: rounded ʊ ɯ x and 3 . V to W is an obvious teaching sequence, but X to Z is not much help. S can be described as a diagonal letter and the sequence S Z S Z S Z S Z is useful to show the opposite directions of the letters.

Most of the faults of the basic S and some of ʃ are caused by the wrong point of entry and direction of stroke. Once the C is correctly written, the sequence C S C S C S and cs ʃ cs ʃ will help. These patterns

can also be used.

There can also be faults in the angle of the main stroke of the letter ʃ. It often bends backwards ȣ Then the sequences ʃlʃlʃlʃl or ʃjʃjʃj or ʃlʃjʃlʃj can help.

The pictorial pattern for this family is

although   or   could both be used.

swan   snake   water

S and ʃ are often much modified in personal cursives. Children may need help in redesigning the letters later on. SS and ʃʃ can be taught as a single cursive cypher. It is seldom successful just to repeat the same strokes.

50

Other useful letter groups

Some letters may change groups if different models are used.

Grouping by letter heights

(1) All ascenders

bdfhkl

   Useful sequences

lhlhlh lflflf dlbldlbl

(2) All descenders

fgjpqy

   Useful sequences

jyjy jygjy quga jfjf pgpq

(3) Letters with no ascenders or descenders

aceinmorsuvwxz

(4) Exceptions

t medium height   f can ascend or descend

   Sequences showing differing heights

itlitl ilj itly fly flit

All circular letters

anti-clockwise   clockwise

cadgqoe   pbk

Exercises

bodobo podapo pgpdpg

Words for spacing

pea pod good bed bad cocoa

Grouping by points of entry

Letters starting from top downwards

b h i j k l m n p r t u y   v w x

   diagonal

Letters starting at top right to left   cfsaogq

Letters starting at top left to right   z

Letters starting in the middle   e l-r   d r-l

Dotted letters   ij ijijij

Letters with crossbars   ft can join fi ti ff tt

Letters which need not join   pb xz jyg and sometimes qs

Letters which join at top   orvw ovov vovo row

Letters which join at base   hilmntu straight acedk round

Letters which can be joined from the left or not as desired.

acdgqoest

acacac or acacac air join

51

16. Spacing

Teachers themselves must understand the principles of spacing letters in a word and words in a line before they can successfully teach children.

A letter is a pattern of strokes, a word is a pattern of letters and a line is a pattern of words.

Legibility requires that the letters in each word are grouped together, and that a sufficient, but not excessive, space is left between words.

Let us take first the space between words. This should be the equivalent to the letter **o** of the size and model being written. Therefore a large round writing needs a larger space between words in order to be legible than a small compressed one. The spaces are proportionate to either the open or dense pattern made by different sized letters and are related to each individual's writing. This is quite easy to explain and demonstrate.

largeoroundowriting   smallocompressedowriting
large round writing   small compressed writing

Unfortunately young children are taught far too often to use thumb or finger as a spacer. At the very best, this may be roughly accurate with the small thumbs and large handwriting of a 5-year-old. It is a simple rule, easily remembered, and it leads to the wide word-spacing so often seen later when thumbs grow larger and writing gets smaller.

Here   is   another

map   of   Cornwall.

Widely spaced words caused by the thumb being used as a measure.

To teach a child at an impressionable age a completely wrong principle even for the sake of temporary convenience can only be harmful in the long run.

uyohmouyohm
nmrhonmrhonmrh
himohumohutohit
hintotintomintolint

Spacing with an **o**. Use corrective patterns, a letter family group, short words or a stroke-related phrase depending on the level that the child has reached.

runotillomyohill

As for the space between letters in a word: to achieve good letter-spacing, which matters more in formal lettering than in handwriting, differently shaped letters require different amounts of space beween them. The space between letters and the space enclosed by letters is as important as the actual shape of the letters in achieving good spacing.

Two round letters need least space, a round and a straight letter a little more, two straight strokes need the most space. This is useful when evolving stroke-related exercises to correct spacing in children's handwriting. It is much easier to see how to correct spacing when the letters of all words in a sentence are made of similar strokes, which then produce an even pattern.

*it hit him   hum until my hymn
in my limit   hunt in my tin hut
try my thin mint   run until I'm ill*

At the cursive stage there may be other problems. It must be understood by teachers and then explained that the joining stroke is also a spacing stroke, so that changing the angle of the joining stroke alters the spacing of letters.

little   little   little

An uneven untidy hand with letters at different angles occurs when the joining strokes of different families are themselves written at different angles.

alone   alone   neither

This occurs most often when children have been taught a variety of different styles. They will need repetitive letter exercises – combinations of all letter families to correct ligature and therefore letter angle and spacing.

Another spacing problem arises in words where some letters join and some do not, e.g. *jungle baby*; again a simple letter sequence can explain and correct this: *junjunjun bababab*

17. Joining strokes

This is not a copy book so I am not proposing to demonstrate the numerous variations of joined combinations that a child needs to be taught and to practise until they become automatic. They are amply illustrated in the many teaching manuals that are available. Anyhow the angle and method of joining, and even the decision as to which letters it is desirable to join, vary from style to style and teacher to teacher.

At one extreme, in the looped styles deriving from copperplate, it is recommended that all letters should join, all the time, including looped descenders and open p and b. At the other extreme, no descenders ever join, nor do p or b, and there are no joins to any of the round family of letters or to ascending strokes. In these cases the same movement occurs, but the pen is lifted from the paper, giving rise to what can be described as an air join. In between are schemes that suggest that the pressure of the pen on paper is reduced in the joining stroke, or that joins are used only when comfortable.

So once again one is torn between teaching children to know how letters can join up correctly, and forcing them into joining all their letters by an inflexible discipline which can be counter-productive. Joins will, in the end, be a matter of personal choice, and children should not be expected to join all possible letters all the time.

It is important to understand how joins are written naturally in a personal hand. In the disciplined flowing copperplate, continuity of letter was achieved by a forearm movement, often without the arm resting on the writing surface. When more of a wrist movement is used, as is usual in modern writing, the whole weight of the arm is resting on the table. Then there must be a break in the writing of a long word for the writing hand to move along the line, or distortion takes place. In a fast adult hand this happens every five letters or so, depending to a certain extent on the amount of lateral space taken up by different sized writing, individual habit as well as the juxtaposition of easy, or difficult-to-join, letters.

Working with my method of flowing separate letters, children should be joining the easy letters of the line-and-arch families naturally as their writing gets smaller and closer together, and their thoughts flow more freely. Then the top joining letters must be demonstrated and practised in sequences such as oooo roro vovo row vow

When teaching 'joined-up' it is desirable that the letters' shapes are based on an oval and at a slight forward slant. This is most necessary where the joining to the letters a c d e g o q s takes place.

The exaggerated use of entry strokes which can lead to over-lapping *int* instead of joining up is uneconomical and does not lead to the desired cursive. The joining stroke as a simple diagonal leads to the many jagged so-called italic hands *int* one sees in junior schools and develops into an illegible zig-zag later on.

think when humming little

Exaggerated entry and exit strokes that overlap and do not join up.

Children who have had the misfortune to be taught several different styles during their early schooling often end up with mixed angles to their ligature strokes. It is often the joining and spacing stroke that is causing the unevenness in writing. Individual repetitive sequences made up of those letters whose joining strokes are causing trouble then help.

This example shows that uneven ligatures cause variation in slant and therefore uneven writing.

As older children develop personal cursive hands more time is spent and individuality shown in the ligatures than in the actual letters. Providing their initial movement and letter construction are correct, this is all to the good. Whether a descending *f*, *g* or *y* joins or not must be a personal choice. Speed and consistency develop best when early disciplined training is followed by encouragement to pursue individuality.

Looking at ligatures

Losing a stroke   Joining to and from round letters

Illegible personal ligatures

Beautiful regular ligatures

55

18. Points to remember in corrective teaching

The first need is for the teacher to have an open mind. It is essential to judge and assess each pupil's problems, seeing what has been caused by poor teaching, what is caused by disability or tensions either temporary or permanent, or later on by rebellion or despair; indeed, what children are signalling through their writing.

An open mind enables the teacher to consider both sides of the arguments for and against different materials, methods and styles. What helps one child may inhibit or handicap another.

Nothing much can be done about such a personal activity as handwriting without a pupil's active cooperation. Therefore everything must be for that pupil's own benefit and not for the good or the image of the school, or convenience, or the teacher's gratification. Furthermore, it is essential that the pupil understands this, so that both teacher and child will be fighting problems from a common point of view.

With this in mind I will try to list the main points to be considered in remedial teaching. Many of these apply also to general teaching.

(1) Explanations

Every pupil from 5 years old to adulthood deserves and profits from an explanation of how the situation has arisen, why it has to be tackled and how it should be dealt with.

How it has arisen Once a diagnosis has been made and some of the practical problems sorted out, it is often necessary to confess, particularly to older children, that they have been badly taught in the past, and that they are not to blame.

Why it must be tackled Pupils, whatever their age, should be helped to understand their present problem in the light of future needs and expectations. From their earliest days at school, children should have an explanation of why, for instance, their faulty letter construction must be changed. A neat clockwise o is just as perfect in the eyes of a 5-year-old as an anti-clockwise one. It is only incorrect in the context of its leading to cursive, and in the ultimate interest of speed. Most young children can understand this if given a demonstration of joined-up double o and perhaps a visual aid to help them remember it. Understandably they will react less well if they are just blankly told that they are wrong.

Another basic fault – an incorrect grip – also needs careful explanation and a practical demonstration of the benefit of changing it. A high degree of personal motivation is usually required to make this alteration, the advantage of which – or rather the disadvantage of not changing it at an early age – is evident only at a much later stage. The need to change from separate letters to cursive again needs careful explanation.

How to tackle it Obviously with young children the initiative must come from the teacher, both in diagnosing and then in evolving, directing and following up exercises. However, quite young children can be very logical and, having been given the necessary explanation and ideas, can profit from being left alone to practise. By 7 or 8, many of the children that I have had for quite short sessions have taken pride in going back to their classes and developing their own exercises. This self-help works especially well with children who are just on the verge of using cursive. Repetitive exercises in a vertical layout are useful and satisfying because they promote improvement and make it evident. It is constructive and non-competitive and helps to develop the necessary critical faculties that are so often unawakened in schoolchildren.

Once a problem has been explained, self-training or retraining restores self-respect and confidence. These are compounded and reflected in the pupil's writing as improvement builds up. The older the pupil, the more important this is. To be in the remedial stream of a secondary school is inhibiting in itself.

Almost all the pupils need flow exercises. These can accurately be explained and described as 'warming-up and relaxing' and compared to training in sport or ballet where there is no stigma attached to such coaching.

Those with multiple learning problems should find that removing the one that is perhaps easiest to cure (handwriting) may help in other areas. An explanation and understanding of his handwriting problems should lead to a more relaxed attitude in the pupil and that improvement should in turn make spelling, grammar and creative writing less of a worry.

(2) Motivation

This is most important in any skill training. Learning handwriting is an unsatisfying exercise if it is not used. In everyday teaching and even more in remedial work it is necessary to arouse and harness the pupil's motivation. This means not only suggesting how to make use of handwriting and explaining its importance in our lives but making children think for themselves how they need and can make use of writing in their own situations. An enthusiastic, imaginative teacher, making a genuine effort to relate to each child's interest, can help enormously.

From an early age, making lists, keeping diaries and records, writing notes within families and cards to absent friends and relatives should be encouraged. This can start with captioned pictures.

Just a little
of toast
and butter
and no jam
or marmalade

Peg a
roBeens
Banana
Cornflakes
Bovrill

A 5-year-old's shopping list and a 6-year-old's menu for breakfast in bed. Examples of young children using their writing at home.

For those reluctant to write creatively and freely, their hobbies, collections and outside interests can be linked to written projects, starting again with lists and captions.

Written games and puzzles at home and at school can be encouraged. Though competition can be a spur to some children, parents and teachers must always be careful not to discourage the less successful. The older the child, the more important self-motivation becomes. As I have said before, retraining handwriting is too important a matter for teachers to impose their own ideas and discipline without active cooperation. The desire for help is usually there under the most rebellious teenage mask. It is often just a matter of finding the right approach.

In my opinion this is *not* achieved by sitting a class of secondary school children down to copy writing cards better suited to 7-year-olds. More resentment and frustration are likely to result. What is needed is a few minutes each session with each pupil, watching, talking and assessing his problems and showing him how he can help himself to solve his special difficulties and develop a more mature hand. This of course means that the teacher needs thorough knowledge of letter forms and remedial teaching exercises, which is the purpose of this section of the book.

(3) Diagnosis

Usually a class teacher will know each pupil's problem and should be able to adapt these exercises to an individual programme, and adjust it if new problems arise. An outside remedial teacher, however, or anyone dealing with a new pupil, needs some sort of diagnostic procedure.

It is important to watch children writing as well as to see examples of their work. Some faults in letter construction, and those of flow, spacing and layout show up in previously written work. To a trained eye indications of children's character and disposition are also evident in their handwriting.

Other faults are only discernible by actually watching a child at work. An incorrect grip, paper position or posture can obviously only be detected this way, and many faults of point of entry and direction of stroke are otherwise extremely difficult to find.

rah   ran   rah   food

This 8-year-old could not join up; his teacher wondered why. The first **a** gives a clue. Watching him write showed that he constructed all his letters from right to left. It took several sessions to retrain his movement.

My method with young children is to ask them to write their names three times with differently coloured writing implements, each with a different sized barrel or handle. This shows me their grip and demonstrates which size writing implement best suits their hands. The repetition shows up which errors are constant and which are just careless slips.

The letters involved in a signature are usually those most likely to have faults in construction. They are learned at an early age, often repeated and seldom corrected so that any errors will have become deeply imprinted and are hard to change. This method of repetition will usually show up which family of letters is causing trouble and provide a guide to which remedial exercises are needed to start with. I usually let children use fibre-tipped pens which flow easily and show both hesitation and pressure points.

Teachers should watch out for any specific strokes that seem to cause a child difficulty. Patterns on the diagnostic sheet on page 40 will help to show if there is a real problem, and practising them may help to correct it. If there is a lasting difficulty, from whatever cause, in forming a certain stroke, children can sometimes be helped to find another form of the letter concerned that they will find easier to write. It is diagonal strokes that are most often the problem.

With older children it may be useful to test them by making them speed up their writing to the point where it breaks up in order to spot their ligature problems.

If a child shows, or suddenly adopts, such marked characteristics as excessively small writing, odd placing of words, unevenness or other signs of tension difficult to control, the teacher or parent should be alert to possible problems in the child's personal life.

How and when pupils break away from a school model or form their own mature hand, is a useful measure of their maturity, independence and willingness to accept new ideas. This may occur at 7 or 8 in an intelligent child or not until 15, if ever, in a really slow learner. In the case of these remedial pupils this may signal a useful, and perhaps last, chance to help them achieve some sort of maturity in thought as well as handwriting.

(4) Demonstration

Teachers should demonstrate with the pupil's own implement on his own paper. Working from a blackboard, transposing from another plane, can be difficult for children, and the arm motions of blackboard writing are not the same as the hand movements that children must learn.

8 oz golden   8 0 9 golden   2 0 q fresh

Teachers must be careful of their own letter forms. An unfamiliar **z** confused this child, who may not have known the abbreviation for ounces.

It is essential for teachers to demonstrate with their left hand for the benefit of left-handers however bad their resulting writing may be. All children, right- or left-handers, benefit from seeing a teacher's hand in action at his own desk, dealing with their personal writing problem.

It may be necessary when starting remedial exercises to enlarge a child's writing to clarify a point. An implement with a fatter point can be used and is especially useful where a child has developed very small writing through tension or for other reasons. However, writing should not be enlarged too much or it brings into play different actions and different muscles from those usually needed in writing. Also, over-enlarging can make it difficult for a child to sustain steady, upright strokes.

(5) Relaxing tension

Tension shows up both in the gripping of the writing implement and the pressure of the implement on the paper during writing. The exercises on page 38 are useful for correcting and relaxing the grip and for showing the light pressure that is needed to glide over the paper and produce a flowing hand.

Any of the pattern exercises can be used with young children to take the formality out of early remedial sessions and to create a relaxed atmosphere. Patterns can be incorporated into pictures, strips of patterns can be cut up and made into paper chains or pattern-covered shapes hung up as mobiles, as well as the more obvious decorative uses as

borders on written work
or bookcovers. Any medium
can be used, e.g. finger paints,
wax resist, or clay and
plasticine which have
patterns scratched or
inscribed.

(6) Collaboration

If remedial help is given by an outside teacher, collaboration with the
class teacher is essential to ensure that the lessons learned are carried on
into class work. This is very important when correcting letter
construction. Changing the point of entry or direction of stroke needs
vigilance and constant reminding and encouraging. If my method is
used, the teacher can use the simplified letter-pattern for all corrections
on everyday work.

Older children with problems in developing a cursive hand will also
need help from all their teachers. There may well be a deterioration in
the appearance of written work when children are changing from print
to cursive, but with practice and encouragement this hurdle can be
overcome.

Unless there is collaboration between the remedial and other
teachers, children at this stage are liable to be criticized for untidiness
and thus positively discouraged from taking this important step.

Poorly written creative work can be used as an exercise in
retraining in skill or remedial classes. One risk of doing this too often is
that children may decrease the amount of their creative writing. A small
section, repeated to show improvement, might be better.

(7) Parental involvement

With many primary school children it is most likely that parental
involvement is taken for granted in the case of handwriting difficulties as
with other learning problems. This involvement should not cease at the
secondary level. Encouragement and incentive to practise at home are a
necessary part of any remedial programme. Whatever age the children, it
is obviously desirable that parents should understand the method being
used to help them, and the reason why it is needed.

(8) Size of group and length of session

There is a need to have both a relaxed pupil and to make best use of a child's span of concentration. One-to-one teaching, even where it is possible, may not always be the most successful.

Any simple corrective pattern work in pre-school play-groups is best done in an informal setting. Perhaps the best way of getting the necessary relaxed atmosphere is to let very young children move freely to and from the table without any pressure to join in the collective activity. Unless they are totally relaxed and enjoying themselves, their span of concentration is very short. At this age children learn as much, if not more, from watching their neighbours as from the teacher.

In infant classes any simple remedial exercises undertaken with an outside teacher are best done in the familiar classroom or at least within sight of the class in an open-plan school, otherwise a 5-year-old might well feel too shy or insecure. A few quiet moments may be needed with each child for diagnosis but even this can be managed in a group of two or three. Short sessions are needed, five minutes at the most, with an exercise dealing with no more than one letter family, before a child goes on to the relevant pictorial pattern as a reward. Then the next child can start; and I find this way it usually ends up with everyone wanting a turn, rather than the problem children feeling that they are being singled out.

In the 6- to 8-year-old range, although their span of concentration may have increased, perhaps from five minutes to ten, children are more likely to be distracted by companions. Their problems are likely to differ, so they will learn less from watching each other and are quite confident enough and do better to have short individual sessions in a quiet corner of the classroom or elsewhere.

Of course children vary enormously in temperament and capability. In the top two classes of junior schools any combination of grouping can work. Those who still have problems with letter construction may need one-to-one assistance and are mature enough to profit from it. The most usual problem at this age is that of flow, and small groups work well together after initial explanation and instruction, evolving and practising exercises. Sometimes it works well to set a whole class first flow and then speed exercises and to move around the room helping those who have special difficulties.

In secondary schools group work has its advantages, especially in the first year when coaching is most needed but not always available. Sets of up to six work well together after a quick diagnostic session. The pupils are at an age to rationalize and profit from discussion and from watching their neighbours. Working in a group of relatively mixed ability children with slightly differing problems takes away the inhibiting stigma of being a poor writer. A pupil who has been helped to overcome his own problems can often help a companion, and both profit from the experience. Older pupils, understandably, can be sensitive about their handwriting problems, and any discussion as to contributory factors is obviously better in private. Short, intensive one-to-one sessions may be best, leading to self-training. Time is precious in the crowded school day.

(9) Other methods

In this book I am concentrating on a method involving the physical production and correction of handwriting through pattern and repetitive exercises. There are other ways of helping children to experience letters through their senses. All of these should be explored to help children solve their writing problems and relate to letter shape and movement.

Before a child puts pencil to paper, arm movements in the air can be used to suggest both stroke-patterns and letter forms. Teachers should demonstrate these with their back to the class to avoid confusion. Then letters and patterns can be traced in sand and finger paints.

The children's whole bodies can be involved by their trying to form letter shapes with their trunks and limbs, either standing up or lying down. This can be done alone or, perhaps easier and more fun, working in pairs. A whole class can be arranged in letter-shaped groups of children, or letters can be marked in chalk on the floor and the children encouraged to walk round them.

Solid letters should be handled; plastic sets are easily obtained. Children can make their own out of rolled plasticine, cut them out of paper, or construct them from adhesive shapes. Tracing and tracking exercises of many kinds can work well if used purposefully. Trays with indented letters are available and can be helpful, even old-fashioned stencils can be used sparingly to guide the muscles into movements dictated by letter shapes and enable the less controlled child to achieve a degree of neatness.

Verbal and visual aids will vary from teacher to teacher. Each teaching manual has its own set of similes to suggest movement and pictorial reminders. With problem children it may be necessary to go through several before finding one that they can react to.

A verbal description of the movement such as 'down-up-and-over' can be useful during exercises and it is always worth stimulating the children's imagination and incorporating any of their own ideas into the teaching vocabulary.

In the future, electronic devices may well be increasingly available for remedial handwriting work. However, diagnosis and a personal programme will always be needed. The instruction that comes out of a machine cannot be better than, or different from, the instructions which were programmed into it.

19. Pre-school children

Children vary enormously in their rate of physical development and this is reflected in all aspects of their early learning.

Some children, whether at home or in a play-group, will be trying to write their names and perhaps more before they reach the age of 5. Others are pressured by parents into trying to form letters before they are ready, while others may have been totally neglected.

In the teaching of handwriting the concept of 'writing readiness' is as useful as 'reading readiness' in the teaching of reading. When we are discussing pre-school children, a precise definition is not so important as a recognition of this concept.

To push children into trying to form letters before their hand and eye coordination, and their ability to perceive or copy, are sufficiently developed, causes tension and probably problems later on. Perception, coordination and motivation can all be stimulated by permitting play and pattern.

It is equally undesirable to hold back an advanced child who is ready and wants to communicate in writing.

Teachers often say to me that they find those children who know least about letters when they start school the easiest to deal with, while admitting that the many children who have had no graphic stimulation at home are at an obvious disadvantage. What teachers would like is children with writing readiness who have not had a false start. Whatever the case, it is essential for any adult with pre-school children to realize the necessary pre-writing stages and the importance of correct writing habits from the start. Then any early attempts at handwriting are a help rather than a hindrance when those children enter school.

This is not a good way to start. The adult's capital letters are not even a good model.

Teaching a child to write in capital letters or encouraging and praising a child for writing with wrongly constructed letters can lead to problems that require remedial help as soon as formal schooling begins. Letting a child write with an incorrect grip, particularly in the case of left-handers, is storing up trouble for the future. These are the 'false starts' to which teachers refer.

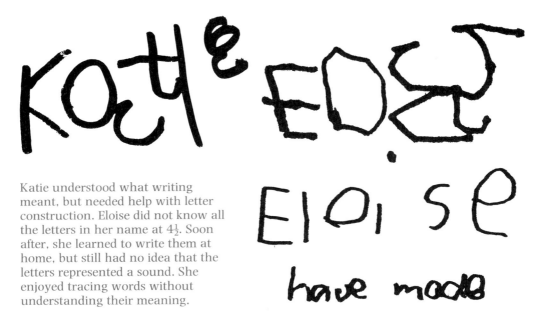

Katie understood what writing meant, but needed help with letter construction. Eloise did not know all the letters in her name at $4\frac{1}{2}$. Soon after, she learned to write them at home, but still had no idea that the letters represented a sound. She enjoyed tracing words without understanding their meaning.

Attention should be paid by all concerned with young children to the check list on pages 14–17, 'Practical factors to consider before starting to write'. This should be circulated to play-groups and, through them, made freely available to parents.

At whatever age a child starts to use a writing implement, pattern is an essential introduction to writing. Pattern can be explored in other media such as finger painting.

The preferred hand may not yet be obvious, but careful observation of how children use their hands in performing tasks that require fine control is often a guide. Tasks such as threading beads and laces, manipulating puzzles, etc., help a child to achieve the finger control and hand-eye coordination that will be needed to write.

The only general rules that I feel it is safe to formulate for parents of under-5s are:

(1) Those wishing to learn to write before starting school should not be held back, but they will need very careful guidance from the beginning to avoid bad writing habits which can be formed as soon as children start to write their own names.

(2) Those not ready to form or perhaps even perceive letters should not be pushed into writing too early. They will profit from free pattern work progressively planned towards forming letters, as well as all sorts of graphic play.

(3) Those less privileged children who receive little or no graphic stimulation, play or pattern work in pre-school years will be at a distinct disadvantage and will require careful help on starting formal schooling before they will be ready to write.

Free pattern for the pre-school child

The work on the following pages was done by children from 2 to 4 years old, in local, unstructured play-groups. Children wandered in and out picking up fibre-tipped pens and learning as much from watching their neighbours as from the zig-zags and spirals that I showed them. I made only verbal suggestions for subjects and uses of patterns. These examples are not meant to create a norm but to show a progression of ideas. The spiral below was drawn by a child of 2 years 3 months.

The all over pattern was drawn by Katherine who was nearly 5.

A correct pencil hold is a prerequisite of free movement so I took the opportunity to correct children who were not holding their implement properly and showed them the improvement in their work. John's first effort at free movement was not successful because he didn't hold his pencil properly. He was shown how to change his grip and produced a good free spiral.

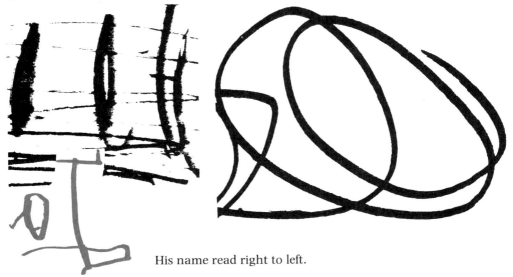

His name read right to left.

Mirror writing

Mirror writing occurs more often in a child whose preferred hand is likely to be left. However, it is quite common at the early stages of writing and often indicates no more than that the child is uncertain where on the page to start writing and in which direction to proceed.

The left-to-right writing movement is an arbitrary evolution in our culture. Right-to-left movement occurs in other alphabets such as Hebrew and Arabic, and is an easier direction for a left-hander to use.

Mirror-writers require clear explanation and demonstration of the left-to-right movement and letter construction and plenty of supervised left-to-right pattern to reinforce the correct direction. They may need the starting point for each line to be marked in some way for a short time, until the correct writing habit becomes natural.

These 4-year-olds only wrote their names in reverse when they started on the right-hand side of the paper.

Pattern into picture

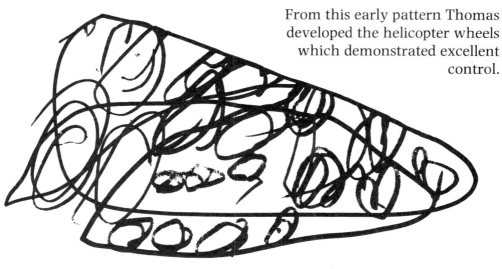

From this early pattern Thomas developed the helicopter wheels which demonstrated excellent control.

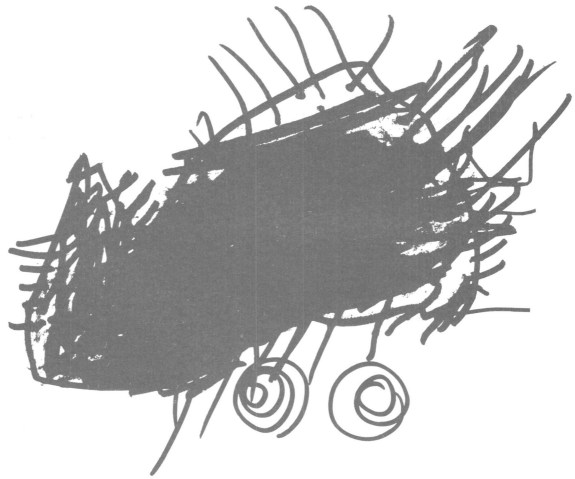

Then a running pattern
then a tractor.

However the free movement is not echoed in the strokes of the letters in his
name which he wrote last of all. The next stage would be to draw his
attention to the relationship between the shape of the helicopter wheels
and the letter o then a.

Charles

Charles wrote a good **h** so it was easy to show him how to correct his **r**.

hnr hnr

I asked each child to draw a star to test their strokes. Then I suggested a few subjects for them to draw and decorate with pattern.

Joan

This child had exceptionally good movement in her patterns
and drawing but I fear her reception class teacher will
have a lot of problems with her. She had obviously
been praised for her 'advanced' handwriting and
produced some quite lengthy written examples
for me to see. All her letters were wrongly
constructed and she resisted all suggestions
about correcting them.

20. 5- to 6-year-old children

When children enter school at 5, they are not only at differing stages of learning how to write but at widely different stages of graphic development. This involves perceptual ability as well as coordination.

Some children may be able to write their names, others even more advanced may be starting to express themselves in writing. Some may have been pressured into trying to form letters before they are capable of it. Most of these children will have developed one or more bad writing habits of construction or grip which will require careful correction. Other children may have had little or no stimulation and need a great deal of help and pattern work before starting to write actual letters.

The moment children enter a normal teaching situation is vital. Assessment must be made of their writing readiness, and their errors must be diagnosed and remedied before they become more ingrained. The right movement and method must be taught from the beginning.

Perhaps I can define 'writing readiness' more precisely here: The perception of pattern, possibly the awareness of the relationship between pattern and letter, an awareness of direction and the beginning of a copying capability, sufficient hand-and-eye coordination and span of concentration and a desire to express or communicate. Each of these can be stimulated in a relaxed atmosphere.

Perhaps it would be helpful to define the differing levels of perception of pattern leading to the recognition and use of letters – those arbitrary patterns of strokes to which we assign sound and meaning:

(1) The visual perception of pattern alone.

(2) The perception of pattern with meaning – such as pattern-making, a meaningful drawing or simple recognition of the pattern of lines making a letter.

(3) The perception of pattern representing a sound, when a child understands that the pattern of strokes that make up a letter also represents a sound.

With all these points in mind, it is easier to judge when a child is ready to write, or where the difficulty may be in a late developer.

Once the practical problems dealt with on pages 14–17 have been sorted out and the correct grip explained and individually demonstrated, the first exercises that may be needed are those to relax tension causing undue pressure on the writing implement or on the paper. These are the same exercises that can be used when correcting a poor grip and appear on page 38.

72

Showing the development of an **e** from spiral patterns.

Pattern is all-important for teaching pencil control and the right movement for constructing letters, pages 39–41. However, pattern needs just as careful teaching and supervision as actual grip writing. Unless the point of entry and direction of stroke are right, the pattern exercises, used as pre-writing skill training, can be counter-productive, confirming an incorrect movement instead of teaching a correct one. Pattern can increasingly be based on letter shapes until repetitive letter sequences can take its place.

All teaching, whether dealing with letters demonstrated as movements in the air, traced in sand or written, should be in stroke-related families and not taught alphabetically or phonetically. In this way the correct point of entry and direction of stroke are repeated and reinforced. The teaching cards on pages 42–3 can be copied by teachers into the class model and used for practice, and to ensure that children master the simplest group before progressing to the next.

Teachers must find a way of one-to-one teaching, if only for short periods. Young children learn best from seeing a teacher demonstrate with the children's own implements on their own paper. Left-handers especially need this, with the teacher initially demonstrating the grip with the left hand.

Copying from a blackboard is difficult for most young children, since it involves transposing from a different plane, trying to remember and copy from a different scale and arm movement. Unless a teacher actually watches a child write it may be difficult to detect individual writing errors.

It is important to make sure that all the children fully understand the language of writing. Words such as 'curved' and 'straight', and even 'up' and 'down' may need to be demonstrated.

It is to be hoped that teachers using the method suggested in this book will consider the advantages of switching from a static print to flowing separate letters. Whatever alphabet is used, however, teachers individually, and in different groups within the same school, should be consistent in their own writing whether on the blackboard, in display notices throughout the classrooms or in any written teaching material.

Cooperation between teachers and parents on the subject of handwriting, as with all aspects of early teaching, is an obvious advantage.

Children vary greatly in their capability, their opportunities and even their motivation towards writing. Their attitude and progress can be influenced by their own parents and their schools' priorities. It is almost impossible to set a 'norm' or average for any age. It is far better to have, especially in the early years, a progression of stages through which each child should pass at his own speed. With good teaching, those who simply lack pre-school stimulation should soon catch up.

Slow progress can, of course, be the result of late physical development, or equally of disadvantage, or a recognized or unrecognized handicap. Teachers will have to be alert to all these possibilities and it is not always easy to judge what is causing the problem indicated by the slow learning of handwriting. However, poor teaching and a laissez-faire attitude to handwriting will leave all these children progressively worse off. A stage-by-stage teaching method with an imaginative approach to stimulate slow learners, and clear explanations and exercises that will help to solve some of the problems of those with multiple learning difficulties, will be an obvious advantage to all. Then those few children with complicated writing or multiple problems will soon stand out, and, in my opinion, the earlier they get specialized help the better.

In this section of the book I am trying, therefore, to show the most usual problems of each age group with suggestions of how to deal with them.

A 5-year-old demonstrates most effectively the use of writing patterns in artwork.

Here are two examples of the work of 5-year-old boys, written towards the end of their first year at school. Their situations are as similar as possible, both being the youngest of large families, intelligent, musical and, as it happens, friends.

The first family concentrated during pre-school years on teaching their son music (notice the letter b formed like a treble clef). His writing shows typical beginners' faults, with wrongly constructed letters as well as capital letters, though his use of language and spelling are well above average.

The second example is that of a boy whose mother is an experienced teacher of writing. He was encouraged to write from 3 years old at home and at kindergarten. His writing is exceptional for a 5-year-old. His own capability, enhanced by early, informed teaching, clearly shows. I am not suggesting that every 5-year-old could do as well with one-to-one teaching. Joining up letters needs maturity of thinking as well as coordination. However, I feel that children's capabilities are often underestimated. If it is properly taught from the start, handwriting need not be difficult; to the contrary, it is a satisfying skill. The responsibility for laying the foundation of good handwriting rests with the child's earliest teachers.

Pattern into letters

Illustrated by the work of
5-year-old children.

Clockwise and anti-clockwise arches **n** and **u**
movement can be explained as the rough or
smooth waves on the sea. A good letter can be
isolated and a boat drawn as a reward.

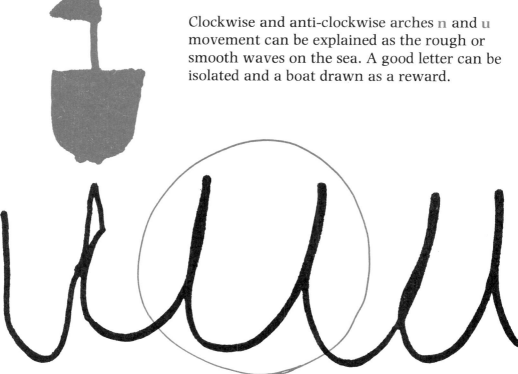

The next stage illustrated by the same child.

It is not always as easy to establish correct movement.

Letters from his signature show that this child can manage round letters but needs help with all line and arch letters.

The exercise for him

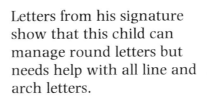

then perhaps

(the school's model).

Many children enter school at 5 totally unstimulated. Perhaps, like this child, they use left or right hand indiscriminately. She picked up her coloured pens with whichever hand was nearest. The jagged strokes produced by her left hand indicated that most likely her right hand was dominant.

Left hand

Right hand

She did not know up from down so teaching her to start her strokes at the top was difficult. She did not react to any of the usual visual ideas such as a bouncing ball or falling rain, nor could she understand the use of a coloured dot as a starting point. Finally I drew a line, called it a washing line with socks hanging down from it and she grasped that at once. Surprisingly she had no trouble thereafter starting alternate short and long strokes from the top.

She finally progressed from pattern to some recognizable letters. She needed that satisfaction but it would be a long time before she caught up with the class where most of the children could already write out their daily news.

Other children start school requiring remedial exercises to correct faults in letter construction. With a little individual demonstration and explanation they should learn quickly at this age.

This child's teacher had not corrected her **as** but she had no trouble in understanding how to change them.

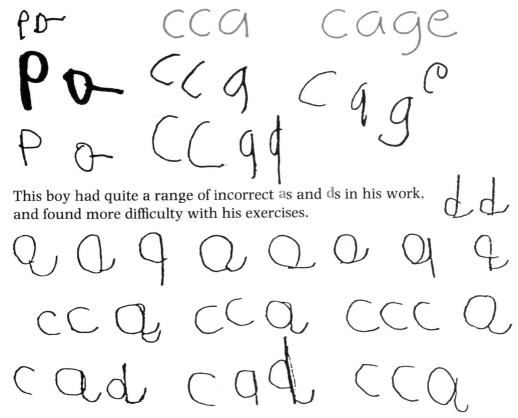

This boy had quite a range of incorrect **a**s and **d**s in his work, and found more difficulty with his exercises.

He eventually understood but needed more help and practice.

This child's problem had arisen from copying lines of letters in alphabetical order from typeset sheets. She understood at once what was needed.

Flowing separate letters by 5-year-olds

One school in my area has introduced flowing separate letters instead of print script to their infant class. These children, nearing the end of their first year at school, show that, whatever the standard of their writing, they find little trouble with a joining stroke.

in ininin

mummy

Although this child still uses static letters to write her name other letters are flowing and well controlled. She finishes her descenders with a flourish. All that needs correcting is her letter o.

not in my house

my cat is

a litte cat

Her pages are covered with pattern.

him   inini

ihuhu

cacaca

cacaca

cdcdcd

cdcdcd

This child also uses straight letters in his signature and flowing ones for other words. Although his writing is small he has little trouble with either movement or joining strokes. He asked to do his exercises in boxes.

cca   ccd   dad   adadad

ccc   ccd   dad   adadad

Faults were usually those of wrong construction, and corrections were not complicated by the joining strokes. On the contrary, these strokes were usually neater and more natural than those of 7-year-olds being retrained from a static hand.

Reversed ds dealt with by exercises.

These children should have very little difficulty in developing a cursive hand as soon as they are mature enough.

Again straight letters in the signature. Incorrect m, u and d show up when writing the words mum and daddy.

A new child still writing her name in capital letters soon gets the idea.

Exercises work quickly on 5-year-olds.

This child had several faults. First I tackled his round letters, then used the sequences to demonstrate the spacing of letters and words.

cccoOccraOcccd

ccco ccca cccd

Shutothat Odoor

Sbut that door

This 6-year-old child had an unusual movement problem with round letters. His writing was also very small.

and met and then you put them into around and

Exercises similar to those above soon showed him the right movement, and thicker fibre-tipped pens encouraged him to write larger.

there was a little girl

one day the little girl

In his next story he made a fairly good start but soon deteriorated. It is relatively easy to retrain with exercises, but it takes a long time for the improvement to show consistently in creative writing work.

the Beaker and and

woof Brok inte the ne

The 'ands' become worse and worse as the child gets more involved in the story.

and and and

Tony's signature showed he had developed a strange y. This was not very good when y came at the beginning or middle of a word. Here are the four separate stages of redesigning his y. It was surprisingly difficult for him.

Stage 1

Stage 2

Stage 3

Stage 4

The exercise *ujuyujuy* might have helped.

21. 7- to 8-year-old children

By 7 years old children should be starting to join up their letters. Not only are they normally ready to think of words as a whole, but if they are to attain a relatively fast flowing hand by the time they leave primary school time should not be wasted.

It is at this stage that the shortcomings of early teaching and style become apparent. Letters that are wrongly constructed cannot join up, and those children who are confirmed in, and often over-praised for, a neat static print, frequently find the most difficulty in changing to a different writing movement.

Remedial exercises are therefore needed to correct directional fault in the letters, which by now may be hard to detect and need careful observation by the teacher. Conversion from static print to cursive profits from repetitive intermediate exercises in separate flowing letters to help change the basic writing movement.

Some manage better than others.

None of their joining strokes looked as natural as those of children who had been taught a flowing hand at 5, and it would be some time before these children became consistent in their daily written work.

This child was sent to me for one short session. She managed to adapt quite quickly and went on alone to develop these exercises into simple cursive.

The more difficult ligatures leading to the round family of letters need careful teaching and practising until they become automatic; also those letters that join at the top. The letter r may need to be altered to r.

A child of 8 with faults in letter construction may find considerable
difficulty in correcting them.

This girl's signature shows that she had a static
hand with her line and arch letters starting at the
base. They needed to be corrected first in a print
sequence for her and then in flowing separate
letters before she could attempt to learn cursive like
the rest of her class.

A sequence worried her, so we concentrated on *in*. Lines helped her.
Writing 'him' proved difficult so we went back to separate letters.

Then I explained that joining strokes are also spacing strokes and
eventually she achieved an **m**.

She would need encouragement and practice with such sequences as:

Two Julies show the problem of joining up the letters in their name,
which they had both been previously writing in separate letters.

They both have trouble with
letter height. These exercises
should help them.

Training a whole class in a definite style may be to the teacher's
advantage at this stage where discipline and practice are so necessary.
However, before the end of this period, strong characters will have
started to assert their personal style. This is to be encouraged once the
correct writing movement and flow are established, and should not be .
regarded as a tendency to indiscipline or defiance.

22. 9- to 11-year-old children

Any of the problems of the previous age group can still be hampering children's progress and need correcting at a time when the emphasis should be on speeding up handwriting and developing a natural style.

To those still keeping to a fast print or separate letter alphabet it must be explained that, although initially there will be a 'deterioration' in tidiness and no immediate increase in speed, both will improve with practice, and in the end it is greatly to the pupil's own advantage to make the change. Self-motivation is essential at this age – and any correction must be honestly explained in the context of its being of help to the individual concerned. Flow exercises are helpful – in fact there are few who do not profit from them.

This home
In uniform

This home, and
In uniform

This lively 10-year-old was showing me that joined-up could *never* be as fast as print. He needed help with his ligatures.

An additional problem will be what sort of ink pen or writing implement to adopt. Some schools have rigid rules, particularly when teaching italic. Undoubtedly some children profit from the discipline of a broad-nibbed pen; for others it is a distinct disadvantage. If used at the wrong angle, broad-nibbed pens can cause difficulties to both right- and left-handers. Where ink pens are compulsory, children should at least be encouraged to experiment with the variety of interchangeable nibs available at most good stationers' to find one to fit their individual requirements. But a good letter is a good letter whatever implement is used. Fibre-tipped pens can be used successfully, particularly by left-handers who have trouble smudging their work.

Fell down a well,
his collar bone,
ell never gosneara well

ululldd
ininin
ororo
with mere want

This left-hander needed exercises to help him master an italic pen.

Although I personally do not much like ball points for younger children, it must be accepted that a great many pupils are going to switch to them as soon as they reach secondary level, so it is not inappropriate at least to allow children to compare the results of writing with different implements while they still have guidance with their handwriting.

This is my writing with a ballpoint pen.

This is my writing with a fiber.

This is an ink pen the one I use at school

A 10-year-old experiments. The italic nib will not speed up, the fibre tip will.

I am running fast   I am running fast

I am running fast   write fast

Faster writing showed up his faulty **o** which had to be altered.

how   goosday   goodday

OOOO   how how   good

At this stage, some children may need help in redesigning some of their letters, particularly if they have suffered from being taught in a variety of styles. The letters s and f, and particularly ss and ff, most often need help. Showing the variety of adult letters and ligatures helps the developing pupil to add to and subtract from the school model, improving an immature hand and speeding up writing with personal ligatures.

bicycle is balance   when he had only been
this it becomes ear great wind arose and, lift
difficult and you carried him far across the
practising enough a spider's-web.

Two very different 11-year-olds' writing. Both may need modifications to write at speed.

Occasional speed tests will help to show up the deficiencies of handwriting at note-taking speed and will help pupils to prepare for the next stage of their school life.

23. Secondary school problems

The changeover from primary to secondary education marks a change in the school's attitude to handwriting. It is now expected that most pupils can write adequately, other than those whose multiple learning problems will probably confine them to remedial groups for some time.

But poor handwriting is no respecter of intelligence; many otherwise excellent students will find that the handwriting teaching they have had in junior schools is inadequate, and that their hand is neither fast nor legible enough for note-taking and essays. Their writing is a handicap, a constant visual reminder of inadequacy which is often not their own fault.

Just when children need expert help there is often no provision for it. It is not productive for secondary school teachers simply to criticize children for untidy handwriting. If the junior schools have failed in their task, then the pupils need careful assessment and diagnosis followed by informed assistance. They will first need help in small groups to correct faults of construction and possibly grip, which by now are deeply ingrained, and then in speeding up and possibly restyling immature hands. Those needing help are likely to fall into one of the following categories:

(1) Those not yet joining up their letters – usually because of wrong construction or grip or having been kept too long on static print.

(2) Those not secure and practised enough with their ligatures, who may well revert to print.

(3) Those who have been taught a variety of styles and whose letters may be at differing angles with an assortment of shapes, from round and upright to oval and slanting.

(4) Those who have been trained in an unsuitable style or have followed too closely the school model and who are now, with untidy results, trying to develop a personal hand.

(5) Those often highly intelligent children who developed a personal shorthand, sometimes quite young when they had become impatient with print. Because of incorrect movement, their ligatures and modifications at speed make unfamiliar symbols with a resulting illegibility for teachers and examiners.

Combine any one of these factors with teenagers' changing moods and developing characters, which will be mirrored in their writing, and it becomes clearer why they need help.

This pupil entered secondary school still writing separate letters. This is an early attempt to join up.

*A signal to his hand,
iked to the edge of
raft and peered down
he cage-top curiously
hartenedin the glow of*

Recognizable ligatures must be taught. Exercises soon sorted out most of the problems.

*How doth the little crocodile
Improve his shining*

However, joining to **s** and round letters was still difficult. Maybe this pupil should not join to those letters, but should lift the pen before writing them, i.e. use air joins.

his claws fishes comes

Practical factors can still hinder progress. This drawn out writing was explained by watching the pupil write. A right-hander, he placed his paper to his left side so he could not see what he was writing. As a result he elongated his joining strokes.

*Hollow out a potato
put a strong salt sult
in it and a weak on
order; Primate goes in*

Habits die hard. Even with his paper correctly positioned he found it hard to change his **r**.

*rorororororororororororo. fir fit fi
rorororororo re re re re re re re
green. red red. red. controlled*

89

To criticize a pupil's writing at this age is to criticize his whole person – so the approach should be more careful.

Once the practical problems, which can be as relevant at 15 as they are at 5, have been sorted out, these pupils profit from the same method as younger children do. If their letter construction is still at fault they may need an explanation and demonstration in flowing separate letters, then ligatures before repetitive letter sequences in the problem letter family. These should be cursive.

This 13-year-old needed to go back to separate letters to retrain his **n**. He found it surprisingly hard to change his movement.

If too much emphasis is placed on neatness, there is a risk that the pupil will give up attempts to master cursive and revert to print. A lot of encouragement is needed with an explanation of why a legible, mature cursive is advantageous. Retraining needs plenty of self-motivation.

If their writing is at different angles, then pupils themselves must choose the preferred one. Style is by now a personal matter. However, it is always worth pointing out the advantage of a slight forward slant and oval letters, both for speed and ease of joining up. Some letters may need to be redesigned – most often **f** and **s**. Repetitive letter sequences, with ascending and descending letters, will help to establish a consistent slant.

s and **f** come in all shapes and sizes. Doubling them does not always mean duplicating the letter.

Retraining fs and ss.

Consolidating a style needs the same technique applied to all letter families. Perhaps the most difficult cases to deal with are those with a combination of wrong letter construction who have developed unrecognizable ligatures. They have two stages to unlearn before rebuilding their hand.

This 15-year-old needed help as examination time drew near.

—, the name of a continent representing southward projections from the main mass of

As he speeded up his writing, it fell apart and became illegible.

name of a continent representing the tree southward projections from the main mass of

His **o**'s needed changing, and letters required finishing off properly. Having been shown how, he evolved his own exercises.

o o ooooo or door low row woman
th th th the the the their their

Explaining the technique of repetitive exercises and showing older pupils how to help themselves works very well, and does away with time-consuming and often awkward remedial sessions, depressing in themselves. It provides the double benefits of self-confidence and satisfaction that arise from self-improvement, and that will reflect in the pupils' writing and, one hopes, the content of all their written work.

Suddenly only nhmnhm
old brother was minimum
walking again. chchch church
highly agagaga

This 16-year-old developed his own repetitive sequences to change his rather tense unformed hand. The same sequences show up and then correct faults.

beautiful beautiful beautiful uyuyuy

Poor handwriting is often the result of tension and inadequacy in the less able, but good handwriting is well within their capability. Those leaving school early profit from exercises in letter writing and form-filling. If pupils have trouble with spelling and grammar, they may need to make several drafts of letters or written exercises to sort out these problems. Then they can concentrate on their handwriting.

[handwriting sample]
many times the b take Refuge:
the breachmans for example any
the elegance of to a break in the
possonae gnard bordee again

Not everything concerning speed or legibility can be blamed on the motor aspects of writing – or corrected by exercises. Slow thinkers, whether deep-thinking or not, can only write as fast as their minds work.

Those with fast minds think, and wish to express themselves, faster than their hand can successfully write. Pupils whose examination papers are obviously written too fast to be clearly legible may need practice in planning essays more than they need handwriting exercises. However, tension of mind or muscles can slow down a student's writing at examination time. Plenty of encouragement is needed, rather than criticism, at a time when it is probably too late to do much else to help.

[handwriting sample]
Mary Anderson an American actress
California on the 17th July 1859
an officer in the

This 18-year-old could not speed up her neat upright handwriting to complete examination papers in time. Her grip was at fault. Her thumb and forefinger crossed on her pen, then her hand was twisted at an angle which soon caused pain. A triangular plastic pencil grip dealt with her problems. It enabled her to change her pen hold and write faster.

[handwriting sample]
why why why

Mary Anderson an American

short vacation trip to London resulted
this of these companion watercolours

Schools should be helping their pupils to emerge with legible, consistent, characterful hands, adaptable to the needs of their different lives.

92

Epilogue

Handwriting is a creative activity. It combines the physical production of signs with the expression of a coherent sequence of ideas. By contrast, reading is much less demanding. Yet the teaching of reading is a recognized professional speciality with a comprehensive literature; for the teaching of handwriting there is almost nothing. It is as though the teaching professions had agreed that society will have more use for the ability to receive ideas than for the ability to create and communicate them. This attitude needs to be challenged.

The coordination of intense physical and mental activity which is needed in handwriting is akin to the total absorption associated with the painter or other creative artists. Observe a class of children writing – the concentration can almost be felt. Just as the nature of the artist finds expression in and can be inferred from his product, so does handwriting, including that of children, embody and display the strengths, the weaknesses, the attitudes and degree of maturity of the writer. Handwriting can also indicate the presence of physical or personal difficulty and thus alert the observant teacher or parent to an area where further enquiry may be appropriate.

For the initial teaching of handwriting a model is needed, though not necessarily the same model for every child. The purpose of the model in the teacher's mind is what matters. The philosophy which has informed this book is that the teaching process should not only aid but positively stimulate the growth of individuality. So there will be no surprise that a model is seen not as a fixed 'ideal' style but as a guide to the basic letter form combining ease of flow with legibility, from which the child is soon encouraged to depart.

No tolerable degree of discipline will so suppress a child's character that his handwriting will reproduce the model exactly. But many teachers who would reject that accusation, nurse the ambition which colours what they will encourage or correct or, more important, what they will admire or deplore. Legibility there must be: but to overstress 'neatness' or to make any assessment of content subordinate to presentation can, particularly in young children, prevent development which later may, if they are lucky, enable handwriting to harmonize with personality so that it becomes simple to produce and a joy to read.

Acknowledgements

First, my thanks to my husband John. He not only wrote the epilogue, but with the experience of a career in education, and a special interest in handwriting, has helped throughout this project.

I would like to thank all those who have encouraged me in my work, including Alan Wing, Michael Twyman, Nicolete Gray and Christopher Jarman – and in particular my colleague Gunnlaugur Briem for the cover and so much more.

Then I would like to thank the Kent Education Committee, the heads, teachers and children of the schools where I carried out my research – with a special thank you to Audrey Ellender for her advice and assistance.

I would like to express my gratitude to the many friends who have lent me examples of their children's or in some cases, their grandchildren's handwriting; and also to Walter Strachan for the beautiful samples of italic handwriting by his former pupils at Bishop's Stortford College.

Last, but not least, my grateful thanks to Olive Kitchingman who deciphered and typed my manuscript, and to Elwyn and Michael Blacker who have helped me to see this book through to completion.

Index